MW01611184

Praise for
Worship Vitals

"On the one hand, *Worship Vitals: Signs of a Healthy Worship Culture* by Zeb Balentine is a brief theology of Christian worship practices. It discusses the elements of worship prescribed in Scripture that are necessary for churches to achieve healthy, thriving worship for the glory of God. On the other hand, it is an immensely practical book that can be used by church leaders to move their churches to greater health. Read it for edification. But read it as well for application."
—Dr. Thom S. Rainer, Founder and CEO, Church Answers

"*Worship Vitals* hits the mark in overviewing necessary doctrines and practices of biblical worship. This book can be a catalyst for your worship team and congregation to grow in their understanding and appreciation of true worship. Use it to help unify your people and lead them to worship God in spirit and in truth!"
—Dwayne Moore, Founder of Next Level Worship International; Author of *Pure Praise: A Heart-Focused Bible Study on Worship*

"In *Worship Vitals* Dr. Zeb Balentine frames the critical components of what's needed to build a healthy worship culture as well as any worship-leading author I've read in a long time. I recommend *Worship Vitals* to all worship leaders who are serious about growing in the Word of God, maturing in the faith, and leading their gathering times with rich, devotional purpose.

In our day, worship has become a church phenomenon with its own expectations and standards for presentation quality, but sometimes the basics of what really matters to God in worship gets lost. Balentine, as a worship leader himself, gives some pretty straight talk to his ministry peers on a number of issues that are front and center in the evangelical movement—some theological, some philosophical, some practical. While not every leader will agree with every ministerial opinion of the author, this work effectively targets the areas that really matter in worship today. It calls for personal and corporate emphasis on life-giving biblical values—and devotional ministry that is deeply purposeful.

Thus, *Worship Vitals* is one of those books that every worship leader needs to embrace for personal growth and development of a healthy congregation."

–Dr. Paul Rumrill, Director of the Center for Music and Worship, Liberty University

"The priority of worship as the source and summit of the Christian life requires clergy, church musicians, and lay leaders to reflect on what signs point to a healthy worship culture and what strategies need to be deployed to encourage establishing and maintaining such crucial culture in the local church. In *Worship Vitals: Signs of a Healthy Worship Culture*, Zeb Balentine has complied a most helpful guide to analyzing and implementing biblical worship practices and expressions that form worshipers into Christlikeness. This active participation of our becoming like Jesus the Christ through worship is at the very core of discipleship. In feasting on and obeying the living Word of God and experiencing his real presence at the Table, we become Christ broken for the life of the world. Nothing is more important than that. Dr. Balentine's love for God and his passion to see God's people adopt practices of right worship is evident and clear."

–Dr. James R. Hart, President, Robert E. Webber Institute for Worship Studies

"As a former music minister and current senior pastor, I spend Sunday mornings worshiping with my church family and the rest of the week wondering what went well, wrong, and everything in between. Zeb's excellent book, *Worship Vitals*, stopped me in my tracks, forced me to hit the pause button, and knocked a lil' more sense into me. Worship isn't just the songs we sing on Sunday, or even the service, but a whole-life posture and purpose as God's people. Sure, I knew that . . . but I did not always live it. *Worship Vitals* helped me recapture this mindset, and for that I am eternally grateful."

–Matt Henslee, Pastor, Mayhill Baptist Church, Mayhill, NM; Author of *Jonah Over Coffee*; Co-host of *Not Another Baptist Podcast*

WORSHIP VITALS

SIGNS OF A HEALTHY
WORSHIP CULTURE

Dr. Zeb Balentine

Worship Vitals: Signs of a Healthy Worship Culture

© 2021 Zeb Balentine

ISBN: 978-1-948022-22-4

Rainer Publishing
www.RainerPublishing.com
Spring Hill, TN

Printed in the United States of America

To Michelle.

Everything I do is made possible by you
and the Holy Spirit.

Contents

Preface

Why Worship VITALS? Just like a doctor performs a routine checkup on a patient, observing their vital signs to determine whether they are a healthy person or if they have some health concerns, every church has *worship* vitals. These are vital functions of the worship life of the church. Just as every person needs a routine physical evaluation, every church needs a routine spiritual evaluation to measure how each of their worship vitals are functioning. This will help indicate if they are spiritually healthy or if they have growing health concerns.

I wrote this book because I have a heart and desire for churches to develop and foster healthy worship cultures. God desires and deserves our best efforts in our worship expressions. Finding a game plan to develop a healthy worship culture is very simple. All we have to do is worship in the ways that God has prescribed in the Bible. To be clear, I don't fully subscribe to the regulative principle of worship (worshiping in all of the ways and *only* the ways God has prescribed in the Bible). I believe that God permits a certain amount of freedom in our worship. But I do believe we are to take seriously what God has prescribed for our worship. That's what I seek to do in this book. I'm attempting to bring those things out of God's Word and draw attention to them. Perhaps you can use this as a manual for how we want to shape our church's worship culture.

It is my prayer that pastors, worship leaders, worship team members, and worship students would read this book, be blessed by it, and catch the vision for a healthy worship culture.

Chapter 1
Why a Healthy Worship Culture Matters

When discussing why a healthy worship culture matters in the life of a local Christian church, I think it is important to be clear on what I mean by "worship." Even better yet, what is a "worship *culture*?" Let's first look at what it means to worship.

What Is "Worship"?

If you ask one hundred people to define worship, you are likely to end up with one hundred and one definitions. I've come across several very good ones. For example, Webster's Dictionary defines worship as "reverence toward a divine being." Harold Best defines it as "the continuous outpouring of all that I am, all that I do, and all that I can ever become in light of a chosen or choosing god."[1] Wayne Grudem calls it "the activity of glorifying God in His presence with our voices and hearts."[2] Evelyn Underhill defines it as "the total adoring response of man to the one Eternal God, self-revealed in time."[3] Mike Harland defines it as "our only reasonable response to God's revelation."[4]

Because I'm one person, and I'm writing on defining worship, I feel the need to add to the white noise with my definition of Christian worship: "our correct response to Who God is and what he has done." I'm quite certain I heard that from someone long ago and stored it in my sub-consciousness. So, I'm not claiming that definition to be original with me.

If we look to the Bible, some of the words used for worship help us to form an accurate picture of what worship is. For example, the Hebrew word *shachah* means "to kneel, stoop, prostrate oneself, or throw oneself down, in reverence."[5] *Shabach* is a worship word meaning "to shout to the Lord."[6]

New Testament Greek words for worship help as well. *Proskuneo* is a word that means to "express deep respect or adoration with words or by bowing down."[7] Also, *Sebomai* means "to revere."[8]

The English word for *worship* comes from a form of the word "worth-ship," meaning to ascribe worth to someone or something that is worthy of reverence and honor.[9] So, in a sense, when we say we worship God, we ascribing worth to Him. Just like when Psalm 96:8 tells us to "Ascribe to the LORD the glory due His name."

Now, we ascribe worth to many things: cars, houses, groceries, dollar bills. That's not idolatry in and of itself, because it is not the kind of "worth" that we are talking about with the Lord. God has a significant worth. A spiritual worth. An eternal worth. He alone is worthy of true praise, honor, and glory.

What Is a Worship Culture?

It's impossible to lead a church to have a healthy worship culture if we don't understand what that means. Most people describe their worship culture by the style of music such as "traditional," "contemporary," or the ever-so vague, "blended." Though worship culture certainly does include a church's style of music, it goes far beyond that. There is so much more to worship than a particular style of music. To sum up a worship culture simply by musical style is to have a shallow and underdeveloped understanding of the life and identity of your local church.

The following questions will help to figure out your church's worship culture is:

- What is the theological content of the songs that we sing?
- Are we expressive or more reserved in our worship practices?
- What are our views on and practices of the Lord's Supper?
- What are the church's core values as it pertains to the worship in our gatherings?
- Do we practice private worship?
- Are we multi-generational, or do we have a predominant age demographic?
- How do we include elements such as giving, Scripture reading, and prayer into our worship gatherings?
- Are we more liturgical or more free-flowing?
- Do we have a "stand and greet" or a "passing of the peace" and do we understand why we do or don't do those things?
- How much time is devoted to worshiping through preaching?
- What is the pastor's preaching/delivery style?

- How is the church urged to respond to the sermon (invitation, singing, communion, dismissal/charge)?

This certainly isn't an exhaustive list of questions, but it does help one to see that there is more to a worship culture than a musical or stylistic preference. The reality is, there is no way to accurately define a church's worship culture simply by a term such as "blended." Nor should it. There are so many elements of worship to consider being part of your church's worship practice.

Why Does It Matter?

Because We Were Created for Worship

God, in his infinite perfection, could have existed just fine all alone, in perfect fellowship with the members of the Godhead. Instead, because of his good pleasure he chose to create things ... *all* things. Harold Best says, "Even in His satisfying completeness, God decided not to keep Himself to Himself."[10] He demonstrated his creativity and his omnipotence by speaking beautiful and vast galaxies into existence. He has made planets and stars that will never be seen with the human eye. He has made microscopic beings that went undiscovered for most of human history.

Why did he do this? So they can display His glory and splendor. The psalmist states that "The heavens declare the glory of God, and the sky above proclaims His handiwork" (Psalm 19:1).

Colossians 1:16 notes that not only was everything made "by" and "through" Christ, but all things were made "for" Him. What does that mean? All things were created to bring him delight, to bring him glory, and to worship Him. God sets this tone in the Bible when describing the creation story. After every day of creation, God declared his work "good." God himself acknowledges how awesome and incredible he is.

Now, for us, this would be arrogant and sinful. But God has every right to brag on himself. If you are preexisting, eternal, all powerful, and you create the universe with the command of your voice, then you have every right to brag on your own greatness for all eternity. That's what he's doing here. He's leading by example. He's showing all of creation how they should respond to his acts of creation. Our proper response is awe, wonder, and praise.

The creation of man was a unique act. God created man in his own image (1:27), and instead of creating Adam with his voice like everything else, he "formed" (2:7) Adam like a potter forms the clay with his own hands. When he had finished, God didn't declare this act as "good." Instead, he declared it as "*very good*." This was special. God was setting this act aside from all other acts of creation.

Again, why? The answer is for God to be worshiped. Isaiah 43:7 notes that he created every person for his own glory. Psalm 95:6 says, "Oh come, let us worship and bow down; let us kneel before the Lord, our Maker!" It's not accidental that this verse calls humanity to worship God not only as a generic term but to worship God as one of his specific titles—Maker. It's a reminder of the reason we are made. In order to fulfill our purpose of being created, we will worship the Creator.

Psalm 150:6 says, "Let everything that has breath praise the LORD!" When God breathed the breath of life into the nostrils of Adam (and therefore all of us), it was certainly so that life within us can be sustained, but it was also so that we can use that breath to speak and sing praises to the one who made us.

Here's the truth: If we aren't actively, consistently, and individually worshiping God, then we aren't fulfilling the very purpose of being created. We weren't created to be entertained and to live in luxuries and comforts from the cradle to the grave. We weren't created to be distracted by all of life's pointless errands. We weren't created to simply exist until we die. Our very reason for existing is so that God would be worshiped by his creation. What a gift he has given us—the gift of himself!

Because God is Worthy of Worship

God is worthy of worship for many reasons. First, because of who he is. Many of the psalms provide an example of worshiping God for his attributes. Take Psalm 99 for example. Notice God's attributes that he is praised for: hhe is great (verse 2); his name is awesome (verse 3); he is holy (verses 3, 5, and 9), just (verse 4), and righteous (verse 4); he answers when called upon (verse 6–7); he forgives (verse 8) and avenges wrongdoings (verse 8). This psalm certainly doesn't provide an exhaustive list of God's characteristics, but everything that God is, he is perfectly.

God is worthy of our worship because of what he has done. He created everything in existence. That alone gives him the right to claim all worship for himself. He not only created us, but he demonstrated his great love for us by slaying his only begotten Son on a criminal's cross in order that we could be reconciled to him while we were still sinners. he has done countless things he to prove his faithfulness and goodness to us. We could spend a thousand lifetimes counting such things, and it would still not be enough.

God is worthy of worship for what he is continuing to do for us. God the Father is providing all of our needs (Philippians 4:19). God the Son is faithfully fulfilling his role as the head of the church (Colossians 1:18) and the great high priest (Hebrews 4:14–16) who is interceding for us to the Father (Hebrews 7:25). The Holy Spirit continues to guide us in all truth (John 16:13) as we are being sanctified.

God is also worthy for what he will do. He will one day finally destroy any remnants of racism and will unite every tribe, tongue, and nation around his throne as we worship him together (Revelation 7:9). One day his enemies will gather together for one final battle against our Savior (Revelation 16:13–16; 19:19). And Jesus, like the King he is, will come riding in on a white war horse (Revelation 19:11) and will have a tattoo on his thigh (verse 16), and he will defeat this massive army of evil simply by declaring their defeat (verse 21). That's the side that I will be on. He's the one that I choose to worship!

Because We Will Spend an Eternity in Worship

There is no longer a temple made of brick and mortar in which God dwells and where we meet with him. Our bodies are now that temple (1 Corinthians 6:19). Even our bodily temples will one day be no more. This new temple in which we will meet with and worship the Lord is eternal. It is prepared for us in heaven. Second Corinthians 5:1–3 states: "For we know that if the tent that is our earthly home is destroyed, we have a building from God, a house not made with hands, eternal in the heavens. For in this tent we groan, longing to put on our heavenly dwelling, if indeed by putting it on we may not be found naked."

In Revelation 21:1–4, the apostle John further elaborates on this when he says,

> Then I saw a new heaven and a new earth, for the first heaven and the first earth had passed away, and the sea was no more. And I saw the holy city, new Jerusalem, coming down out of heaven from Go, prepared as a bride adorned for her husband. And I heard a loud voice from the throne saying, 'Behold, the dwelling place of God is with man. He will dwell with the, and they will be his people, and God himself will be with them as their God. He will wipe away every tear from their eyes, and death shall be no more, neither shall there be mourning, nor crying, nor pain anymore, for the former things have passed away.

Because Worship Is Everything

If a church doesn't have a healthy worship culture, then it is not fulfilling its very purpose of being established. Many will argue that discipleship is the most important function of the church. In fact, most pastors will say that the Great Commission is the church's first priority. I would say this is due to an underdeveloped theology of worship. Most pastors delegate worship theology to the people who lead the musical portion of the worship service. It would be refreshing to see more non-musical people becoming solid worship theologians and writing more books on worship. It would help fill a void and provide a unique voice on the matter that, sadly, is gaping wide open right now.

The truth is, the Bible has more to say about worship than it does about teaching or discipleship. As a matter of fact, the most frequent command in the Bible is to sing in worship. This is given to us more than one hundred times. Also, the Great Commandment, to "love the LORD your God with all your heart and with all your soul, and with all your mind, and with all your strength" (Deuteronomy 6:5) was given to God's people before the call to discipleship. In fact, in Mark 12 a group of Sadducees are pressing Jesus on theological questions when a scribe spoke up and asked, "Which commandment is the most important of all?" (verse 28). Jesus responds by quoting Deuteronomy 6:5, adding the second Great Commandment of "You shall love your neighbor as yourself." Then in verse 31 He adds this commentary: "There is no other commandment greater than these."

I don't address this to diminish the importance of the Great Commission. When Jesus said, "Go therefore and make disciples of all nations, baptizing them in the name of the Father and of the Son and of the Holy Spirit, teaching them to observe all that I have commanded you" (Matthew 28:19–20), he left us with a good, perfect, and important task. But it was simply . . . a task. We need to understand *why* it was given to us. *Why* do we make disciples? The answer is, so more people would become worshipers of God, and once they know him as Lord, they can grow and be taught to love and worship him more fully.

Notice again, the Great Commandment referenced in Deuteronomy 6. We are given the command to love (worship) God in verse 5, and in verse 7 we are given a commission of discipleship (specifically towards our own families): "You shall teach them diligently to your children, and shall talk of them when you sit in your house, and when you walk by the way, and when you lie down, and when you rise."

Just because the call to discipleship came most recently doesn't mean it's most important. We need to understand that it's simply a means to a greater end—the praise and glory of Almighty God. I've always loved what John Piper said: "Missions exists because worship doesn't. Worship is ultimate, not missions, because God is ultimate, not man."[11] Christ gave us the Great Commission because the entire globe doesn't worship him as he deserves. Worship is the goal and the Great Commission is the means.

Every sober-minded follower of Christ would agree that to neglect the Great Commission is to be man-centered. It is often neglected because churches want to cater to themselves, be entertained, or bow at the altar of nostalgia. Those are easy symptoms to spot and use to diagnose a church or individual as being man-centered, needing to repent and follow the call of making disciples.

On the other hand, when the Great Commission becomes the ultimate thing for a church, that is man-centered as well, just in a different way. Our focus shifts from God and His glory being our primary focus and desire, to a person's soul and/or spiritual development becoming our priority. Anything, other than God Himself, that becomes an ultimate thing (even good things like evangelism), will become an idol.

Jesus left us with what we have dubbed the "Great Commission." But it is simply a roadmap to a greater destination. It is given to us so that we can worship and love God and to teach others to do the same. Worship is the GREATEST Commission.

Discussion Questions

1. How do you define worship?
2. How would you describe the worship culture of your church?
3. What characteristics go into forming a church's worship culture?
4. How does the Great Commission serve to fulfill the Great Commandment?

Chapter 2
Worship God Only

What do you think of when you hear the word "idol-atry"? Like most, we probably think of statues that people pray or offer human sacrifices to. The Hindu religion probably comes to mind, as they have approximately thirty-three million gods. Maybe we think of idolatry as something you find only in primitive societies. Perhaps we think that idolatry doesn't exist in civilized countries, and certainly not in America.

But let's take a look around and honestly evaluate our own worship culture. We, in the United States, can be some of the most idolatrous people on the planet. Consider what a foreigner might think about who or what we worship if they were to visit our country and observe our lives and practices. Would they see all of the restaurant signs and think that our god is our belly (Philippians 3:19)? Would they conclude that our god is our phone? Before we make a decision of whether or not we can do something, we look down at our phone god to check the time or calendar to see if we have permission to do so. Perhaps our god is our television. In many homes there are more televisions than people. If you go into any living room in America, you will see the living room furniture situated around the television, almost like it where an altar. Every month we tithe to our TV god in the form of a cable or satellite bill or a Netflix subscription. We even evangelize for our television god by talking to others about what's new with our favorite shows.

I'm wring this chapter on a national holiday for our country: Black Friday. You know, that holiday that comes after the other holiday in which we are supposed to pause, reflect, and give thanks for all of God's blessings. Black Friday is that special time of year when people are still in such a thankful and content spirit that they leave Thanksgiving dinner early so they can camp out all night at the local Walmart or Target and wake up the next morning to fight and trample each other in their rabid cravings for material possessions.

Idols take on many forms. In fact, the human heart is nothing if not an idol factory. It makes no difference what part of the world you come from, your ethnic or socioeconomic background, or your religious convictions. Idolatry is a universal problem that plagues the heart of every human being.

Worship God Only

The fight against idolatry and for the worship of the one true God is one that is as old as time and will remain until the Lord Jesus returns. The fall of man in Genesis 3 was an issue of wrong worship. Matthew 4:10 records that Jesus himself fought against Satan's temptation to idolatry by quoting Deuteronomy 6:13: "You shall worship the LORD your God and serve Him *only*" (emphasis added).

When God gave Moses the Ten Commandments, it was no coincidence that the first two commandments addressed idolatry. We will address the second command in the next chapter, but look at what God says in the first commandment: "You shall have no other gods before me" (Exodus 20:3). This can also be translated as "no other gods *besides* me."

God compares idolatry with spiritual adultery. In Isaiah 57:3 God refers to idolatrous Israel as "offspring of the adulterer and the loose woman." He uses even more severe terminology, such as in Jeremiah 3:2 where he calls it "whoredom." Isaiah 1:21 laments Jerusalem's spiritual condition: "How the faithful city has become a whore." At one point God raised up the prophet Hosea, and in order to display God's faithfulness to his unfaithful people he instructed Hosea to: "Go, take to yourself a wife of whoredom and have children of whoredom, for the land commits great whoredom by forsaking the LORD" (Hosea 1:2).

God is serious about our love and devotion for him. When we give our hearts to other things, that is a dirty, vile act. It is not something to be taken lightly. It's offensive and dishonoring to God and harmful to us and those around us.

All of the Bible tells the story of God destroying our idols and drawing us back to worship Him. Jesus came to this earth to rescue us from sinful worship, make us worshipers of God Almighty, and restore us back to God's intention of a perfect fellowship with his human creation. God is serious about his worship. He demands it, fights for it, deserves it, and loves it.

Our Jealous God

God solidifies the first two commandments by declaring, "for I the LORD your God am a jealous God" (Exodus 20:5). This attribute of God may stir up confusion in the hearts and minds of some. One might think, "Would jealousy make God sinful?" The great theologian, Oprah Winfrey (complete sarcasm), once posed the question: "How can this God who is all loving and all powerful, why would God be jealous of me?"[12] These are good questions. Ones that we must labor to find answers for if we are to have a better understanding of the character and nature of God and a better understanding of our role as God worshipers.

The first thing that I want to point out is that the Bible affirms many times the attribute of God's jealousy. The next time we see this attribute mentioned is in Exodus 34:14 after the Hebrews were caught worshiping the golden calf. God makes new tablets for the commandments to be written on, and he reaffirms what he said in chapter twenty. But this time he not only declares he is a jealous God, but he states that his "name is jealous." Why? Because his jealousy is part of who he is. It's part of his identity as God.

The Bible mentions God's jealousy many times after that. This attribute is often connected to fire (Deuteronomy 4:24; 29:20; Zephaniah 1:8; 3:8; Psalm 79:5) and to his wrath (Deuteronomy 29:20; Numbers 25:12; Ezekiel 16:38, 42; Nahum 1:2; Psalm 78:58). His jealousy can be provoked (Deuteronomy 32:16, 21; 1 Kings 14:22). He is jealous for his holy name (Ezekiel 39:25), his land (Joel 2:18), and his people (Zechariah 1:14; 8:2). Not only is God jealous *for* his people, but his jealousy can be *against* his people as well (Ezekiel 23:25).

The second thing to know about God being described as jealous is that God is using an anthropomorphism. In other words, he is using human characteristics to describe himself. For example, when we read about God's hands (Isaiah 66:2), fingers (Psalm 8:3), or face (Numbers 6:25), we know that God is invisible (Colossians 1:15), he is Spirit (John 4:24), and he is omnipresent, so he is not limited to a physical body. By God using human terms to describe himself to us, it's like, as I've heard it said, God is speaking baby talk to us so that our little minds can comprehend him. With that said, we can't perfectly understand exactly what God means when he describes himself in this way, but we can gain some amount of understanding.

The third thing to know about God's jealousy is that it is a righteous jealousy. Most of the time when we hear the word "jealousy" we think of something negative. That's because most of the time jealousy is sinful. But there is such a thing as righteous jealousy. For example, no man wants to share his wife's heart with another man. That's because a husband should have a logical and righteous jealousy for his wife's heart. J. I. Packer states: "There is another sort of jealous: zeal to protect a love relationship or to avenge it when broken. . . . This sort of jealousy is a positive virtue, for it shows a grasp of true meaning of the husband-wife relationship, together with a proper zeal to keep it intact."[13] God has this kind of jealousy for our hearts. He wants to share it with no one else. Nor should he.

God's Response to Idolatry

God's response to idolatry in the Bible is often severe. People are struck with famines (Genesis 12:10; 26:1), slavery (Jeremiah 29:14), natural disasters (Jeremiah 44), or even given over to their own idols (Romans 1). Two ways that God has dealt with idolatry that have always vividly stuck out to me both happened in the book of Exodus: the ten Plagues and God's response to the Hebrews worshiping the golden calf.

The Ten Plagues

One of my favorite examples of God responding to idolatry was through the ten plagues on Egypt. Pharaoh refused to bow to God's will and command to release the Hebrew slaves because he himself was enslaved to the worship of false gods and even the idolatry of preserving his own kingdom. The plagues weren't just random events, but each one was God demonstrating his power and sovereignty over all things. With each of them, God was mocking and proving His might over Egyptian gods. Notice each plague:

Water into Blood (Exodus 7:14–24)
The Nile River was the centerpiece of ancient Egypt. Their lives revolved around it. They believed their goddess, Hapi, believed ruled over it. For God to turn the whole river into blood not only greatly inconvenienced the Egyptians, but it also proved that their goddess was powerless.

Frogs (Exodus 7:25–8:15)
The Egyptians also worshiped a god named Heqet, who was the goddess of fertility, and ironically, she had the head of a frog. Causing an infestation of these creatures, was like God was saying, "You like frogs? How about this?!"

Gnats (Exodus 8:16–19)
Geb was considered the god of the earth. Gnats arose out of the dust when Aaron struck the ground with his staff. This, I believe, was to communicate how worthless it was for the Egyptians to worship such an idol.

Flies (Exodus 8:20–32)
This plague was meant to be a mockery of Khepri, a beetle-headed god.

Diseased Livestock (Exodus 9:1–7)
This act was a mockery of many Egyptian gods. Hathor, Amon, Bat, Apis, Buchis, Mneuis, Ptah, and Ra were all gods associated with cattle. For God to strike them with disease would have sent a clear message to Pharaoh that these gods were no match for the one true Almighty God.

Boils (Exodus 9:8–12)
The Egyptians were a very clean people. They bathed quite often, and the thought of their entire body being covered in boils would have been repulsive. Their god of medicine, known as Isis, would have been called upon to remove this affliction from them. Yet, their idol was silent.

Hail *(Exodus 9:13–35)*
Nut, the Egyptian goddess of the sky, should have been able to prevent this plague of hail falling from her domain. But she is powerless and Yahweh proved to be the Ruler over nature.

Locusts *(Exodus 10:1–20)*
The plague of locusts defied two Egyptian gods. First was Osiris, the god of the underworld from which locusts emerge. He was also considered the god who gave life to vegetation and crops, which the locusts destroyed. The second was Senehem. He was believed to have the head of a locust and would also have been believed to be able to protect against such a plague. Yet both were powerless.

Darkness *(Exodus 10:21–29)*
The plague of darkness was a defiance against Ra, the Egyptian god of the sun, and Horus, the god of the sky. Neither of these false deities could thwart the hand of God when he brought three days of darkness.

Death of the Firstborn *(Exodus 11:1–12:36)*
The final plague was the worst. The death of the firstborn was a statement against Anubis, the god of the dead, and Osiris, the giver of life. Both Egyptian gods proved to be helpless in this situation. This plague was much more personal to Pharaoh, as he himself was worshiped as a god, yet he couldn't even save his own son. Pharaoh's firstborn son was heir to the throne and would one day be considered a god as well, but his fragile life taken from him, along with all of the other firstborn sons of Egypt.

These ten plagues proved that Egypt's gods were powerless and worthless, just like the gods we sometimes create and bow to.

The Golden Calf

Exodus 32 is a sobering chapter. It speaks into the spiritual fickleness of God's people and the seriousness of God's response to idolatry.

While Moses was on Mount Sinai, the people grew impatient. Though Moses was absent for only forty days and forty nights (Exodus 24:18), the people had no idea when or if he would return. They approached Aaron, their priest in charge of worship (Exodus 28:1), and said, "Up, make us gods who shall go before us. As for this Moses, the man who brought us up out of the land of Egypt, we do not know what has become of him" (Exodus 32:1)." Just like they couldn't see their leader Moses, they also couldn't see their God. Their faith in the unseen wasn't strong enough, and they wanted a god and/or gods they could see and touch. There is no doubt that this is a remnant of the many generations of Israelites who lived among the idolatrous Egyptians.

When they collected all the gold jewelry from among the people, Aaron made them a golden statue of a calf to represent many Egyptian deities. The people said, "These are your gods, O Israel, who brought you up out of the land of Egypt!" (Exodus 32:4). How blasphemous! Not only are they worshiping other gods, but they are attributing to something else what Yahweh alone has done for them. God declared himself to be the one who delivered them (Exodus 20:2; Deuteronomy 5:6). The people had forgotten about the ten plagues. They had forgotten about the parting of the Red Sea. They forgot about the God of their fathers: "the God of Abraham, the God of Isaac, and the God of Jacob has sent me to you" (Exodus 3:15).

Instead of standing firm and guarding the worship of the people, Aaron complied with their demands and made their idol for them. Then, like a hypocrite, he said, "Tomorrow shall be a feast to the LORD" (32:5). Why would he say such things? Was he feeling guilt and wanted to lessen the offense? Was his theology just as flawed and his heart just as conflicted as the other Israelites? Either way, his statement reveals two things: First, he wanted to serve two masters. Second, he was going to give God their "leftovers." How often does the church do this today? We want to be cozy with the things of the world while also wanting to appear to be Christians? How often do we devote our time, money, energy, and resources into other things, and if there is anything left, we offer that to God? As we will see, true worship doesn't work like that.

Exodus 32:6 states, "They rose up early the next day and offered burnt offerings and brought peace offerings. And the people sat down to eat and drink and rose up to play." For the most part, the description of their worship on this day seemed to be just fine. They rose up early, as many verses of Scripture prescribe. They offered burnt offerings just like Noah did as an act of worship when he and his family exited the ark (Genesis 8:20). They offered peace offerings like Jacob (Genesis 31:54). They celebrated by feasting just like Isaac (Genesis 26:30).

All of these things were scriptural and part of their heritage and theology of worship that had been passed down to them. So, what's the problem? Notice, it says the people "rose up to play." This is not a reference to monopoly or kickball. This includes indecency and improper dancing. God described them as having "corrupted themselves" (verse 7). This is nothing short of an orgy. Acts of debauchery were common in pagan worship. The ancient Greeks had temple prostitutes who were used for worship (1 Corinthians 6:12–20). This was taking place on the day that Aaron had set aside to worship Yahweh. This is the kind of thing that happens when you try to serve two masters or give God lefto-vers—you don't truly worship him. You really can only serve one.

Next, we see that Moses burned and ground up the idol un-til it was dust, then he put the dust into the water supply and made the people drink it (32:20). This seems odd. Why would he do that? They all had to eventually drink some water. Grind-ing the idol up into dust and putting it into the water supply was to remind them that these false gods are nothing. They should not be worshiped. They cannot provide for them. They can be reduced to dust. They certainly didn't deliver them from slavery in Egypt. They surely are not worthy of worship.

The sons of Levi were found faithful to the Lord, and from that day on they were appointed to be the leaders and preserv-ers of the worship practices of the Israelites (32:29). Their first assignment was to kill those guilty of idolatry. This included their brothers, their friends, and their neighbors (verses 25–27). Scripture notes that three thousand men were killed that day (verse 28). Later a plague was sent onto the people (verse 35). We aren't sure what the plague was, but it was some sort of punishment from the Lord because of the idolatry of the people.

Idolatry is a crime against God that he doesn't take lightly. The consequences are often death, disease, famine, slavery, or some other form of God's wrath. God often responds with great severity, so we shouldn't take the worship of God flippantly.

Idolatry and the Church

Though we may never collect our jewelry and make a golden statue, and our worship services may never turn into an outright orgy, idolatry can run rampant in the modern-day church just as well. A church's version of the golden calf can take on many different forms.

Worship/Music Style

It's quite possible to worship your worship. We can do this when we cling to our preferred worship style, be it piano-driven or band-driven music, old or new songs, or stage lighting and projected lyrics. Our tools for worship can easily become our objects of worship. When we are in pursuit of the worship experience rather than God himself, we are guilty of worshiping our worship.

Traditions

Traditions abound in churches. This can be flower arrangements at the pulpit. It can be a certain ministry or program. I've found during the Christmas season our idols of tradition come out in droves. Think about your worship context. Are the sacred cows so plentiful that Jesus can't fit in the manger?

Order of Service

Perhaps you see idolatry in Christian worship in the order of service. Whether your church is highly liturgical or not, the order and flow of the service can become an idol if we guard it as we would a Bible doctrine. We have no order of service outlined in the Bible, so we have the freedom to change things up a bit. If your pastor or worship leader wants to tweak the order of service, give them the benefit of the doubt and try it out. If you're unwilling to do that, then you very well may have made an idol.

Patriotism

Is patriotism bad? Absolutely not. Is it sinful not to be patriotic? According to the culture, yes. According to the Bible, no. Why do Christian churches in America, particularly in the south, have American flags in their sanctuaries? And why do they have patriotic worship services on patriotic holiday weekends? Idolatry is quite possibly the answer.

If patriotism isn't an idol, why are patriotic services the most passionate worship services of the year? If it isn't an idol, why do we bring those elements into our *worship* services? If we aren't guilty of patriotic idolatry, then why do people become so defensive when you even pose the question of it being a possibility?

Your Pastor/Leader

Some pastors and/or Christian leaders have a messiah complex. They think that they know everything that is wrong with a church or organization, every leader before them was an incompetent clown, and they swoop in like Superman (or Superwoman) to save the day. They have all the answers, talents, and gifts and will now be doing things God's way. I've even heard of some leaders claiming to be sinless. And the sad thing is, people buy into that.

While some leaders can have this view of themselves, some churches can have this view of their leaders. They can hang on every word the pastor says without any kind of discernment or fact checking. Some people have done unethical, unbiblical, or even illegal things for their pastor. Some have covered up a pastor's financial misuse, infidelity, or even sexual abuse. Others are guilty of idolatry by remembering a former pastor or leader so fondly that they look to them as some sort of second coming of Moses. If they represent the "good ole days" of a church, then it could be because they are looking through the lenses of idolatry.

Our Response to Idolatry

For a church to have a healthy worship culture, the people must do these things both individually and collectively as it relates to the idolatry that exists within them.

Recognize

You must be able to recognize within your own life what you've allowed to sit on the throne of your heart. This is not easy to do, for our idols often reside within our blind spots. But we must pray for discernment to spot idolatry within our lives, and then we must have the humility to accept the reality that it exists.

Repent

We can't stop at recognizing our idols, though. Recognition must lead to repentance. The rich young ruler was eventually able to recognize the idol of wealth that lived within his heart, but when confronted with the reality he chose to follow that god instead of Jesus, God in the flesh (Matthew 19:22; Mark 10:22; Luke 18:23).

Return

To give our love and devotion to an idol is to withhold it from the Lord. I'm reminded of Jesus's message to the church in Ephesus in Revelation 2:1–7. In the first part of the message he affirms them in several ways. But in verse 4, he rebukes them by saying, "I have this against you, that you have abandoned the love you had at first." Once you've identified your idols and turned from them, work on rebuilding your love and devotion for the Lord. For some, this abandoning of our love and devotion to the Lord has perhaps been a few weeks, and for others it may have lasted for several years. We should be reminded of when we first came to Christ. Jesus was like that treasure hidden in a field (Matthew 13:44) or that pearl of great value (Matthew 13:45–46). We would have forsaken all in order to have the Lord. He is the true prize. May he bring us back to that love we had at first.

Run

There is a reason the apostle Paul told us to "flee from idolatry" (1 Corinthians 10:14). Our hearts are idol factories, and the idols of the world are in constant pursuit of us, so we must run for our lives. Run from them and run to Christ. Every day. All day.

Discussion Questions

1. What are some of the biggest idols in our culture?
2. What are some idols in our personal lives?
3. What are some idols within our church?
4. What comes to mind when you think of God's attribute of jealousy?

Chapter 3
Worship God's Way

I n Christian worship, does "anything go" as long as your heart is in the right place?

The first commandment provides a theology of idolatry in that we are not to worship anything or anyone besides the Lord (Exodus 20:3). The second commandment states: "You shall not make for yourself a carved image, or any likeness of anything that is in heaven above, or that is in the earth beneath, or that is in the water under the earth. You shall not bow down to them or serve them" (Exodus 20:4–5).

There is some debate as to whether or not these are two separate commandments or if they are meant to be understood as one. Because they are similar and both are addressing the issue of idolatry, it seems like verses 4–5 are an exposition of the commandment given in verse 3.

I believe, like most, that they are two separate commandments. But why? Why would these first two be similar? I think there are two reasons for this. The first is since the worship of God is so important, in fact the most important thing, that the first two commandments focused on it to communicate that fact. Second, I believe that we are given two similar commandments on the worship of God because God knew we would be so bad at it. While similar, I believe that they are distinct enough from each other.

While noted in the previous chapter, the first commandment speaks against idolatry and charges mankind to worship God and God *alone*. The second commandment admonishes us to worship God his way and not in any way that is forbidden.

We must remember to whom the Ten Commandments were being written to. The Israelites have lived among the pagan Egyptians for four hundred years. They were used to bowing down to idols. They were used to having physical objects to worship. God is invisible. He is not to be bound to a physical object. He wants us to have a view of him that expands our hearts and minds. This isn't going to happen if we limit our view of God to an object, a place, a particular practice, or an inaccurate version of him.

So, how do we commit idolatry and break the second commandment? I believe there are primarily two ways: 1) worshiping God in a way that he forbids, and 2) worshiping an inaccurate version of God.

Worshiping God in a Way He Forbids

Everyone wants to call their own shots in our worship expressions. It's within our fallen, idolatrous nature to have the proclivity to do so. Scripture is filled with examples of people who have tried to worship God in forbidden ways and reaped nothing but judgment and rebuke.

Cain

The familiar story of two brothers and the first murder in human history begins at a worship service. The two brothers offered sacrifices of worship. Abel brought the firstborn of his flock as a pleasing sacrifice to the Lord (Genesis 4:4). Cain brought a portion of his harvest from the ground (verse 3). God accepted Abel's offering but rejected Cain's. It's commonly misunderstood that the reason Cain's offering was rejected was because it wasn't a blood sacrifice. But we find out in Leviticus 2 that offerings from the ground were perfectly lawful and acceptable to God.

Cain's sin was that he made an offering of worship to the Lord that wasn't heartfelt. Perhaps he was going through the motions. Maybe the worship expressions had simply become routine or memaningless to him. We can only speculate about the nuances of the situation, but it is clear that he wasn't bringing the offering of worship from a heart of worship. We can see this to be true because he murdered his own brother out of jealousy.

Cain's sin was the same as the Israelites when Isaiah and Jesus observed, "These people honor me with their lips, but their hearts are far from me" (Isaiah 29:13/Matthew 15:8). This sin led Cain to be cursed (Genesis 4:11–14), marked (verse 15), and forever wandering away from God (verse 16). And he had to live the rest of his life with the guilt and shame of taking his brother's life in a moment of jealous rage.

We may not ever murder our own sibling over a worship issue, but the root sin in Cain's life constantly hounds each one of us. We all have had times when we go through the motions. We've all had Sundays that we gather out of obligation or routine rather than joyful obedience. We've all had times when we honor God with our lips (or actions), but deep down our hearts are far from the Lord. This is a form of idolatry. This is not worshiping God in the way that he demands or deserves.

Unauthorized Fire

Aaron and his sons, Nadab and Abihu, were consecrated as priests in Leviticus 8. Aaron was the patriarch of a priestly family, a tradition that was to be passed down through his decendants. In chapter 9 Aaron is commanded to offer a sacrifice to God on behalf of his people (verses 1–6).

The preists were to only offer sacrifices with authorized fire. This was a clear command given in Exodus 30:9: "You shall not offer unauthorized incense on [the altar of incense]." Aarons sons clearly disobeyed this command: "Now Nadab and Abihu, the sons of Aaron, each took his censer and put fire in it and laid incense on it and offered unauthorized fire before the LORD, which he had not commanded them" (Leviticus 10:1).

Why was this fire "unauthorized"? The reason is because the fire is supposed to come from God himself (verses 22–24). Nadab and Abihu took matters into their own hands and wanted to do worship *their* way instead of God's way. They paid the ultimate price for their disobedience. Numbers 3:4 records that they died. Their sin was serious enough that God took their lives. They had violated the most important thing in this universe, and that is the worship of God.

The verse notes that they didn't just die, but it adds, "... and they had no children." This was a significant addition to their punishment. Aaron and his decedents were chosen to be a priestly family. They were entrusted to guard the worship practices of God's people. This was a responsibility and an honor that was to be passed down from generation to generation. Because of this foolish and careless oversight, that great honor and birthright ceased for these two when they died.

Disorderly Worship

Everything about the Corinthain church was disorderly. Unconfessed sin was running rampant in the individual lives of the church members, and it made its way into the collective worship gatherings. Many of the believers were holding onto previous habbits from their life before they came to Christ. That is why Paul urged them to "flee from idolatry" (1 Corinthians 10:14).

Their worship gatherings were toxic. Sadly, Paul admonished them, saying, "when you come together it is not for the better but for the worse" (11:17). In this congregation there were divisions among them (11:18), they were not honoring Christ or each other when they partook of the Lord's Supper (20–22), there was an abuse and misunderstanding of the spiritual gifts (chapters 12–14), and they misused the gift of prophesy and tongues (chapter 14).

There was total chaos. It was ungodly, carnal, self-centered, and disorderly worship. Paul exhorts these worshipers (and all worshipers) that, "all things should be done decently and in order" (14:40). We can't have orderly, God-honoring worship gatherings if we are selfish worshipers, wanting to worship our way. When we look to God and what *he* wants for our church and worship gatherings, then we will have unity, order, and joy.

Worshiping and Inaccurate Version of God

In 2006 Will Ferrell starred as Ricky Bobby, a NASCAR driver in *Talladega Nights: The Ballad of Ricky Bobby*. There's a scene in the movie that many have found to be offensive, but I have always interpreted it as a caricature of how we view God. The main character, Ricky, is sitting at the dining room table with his wife, two sons, father-in-law, and his best friend, Cal. Ricky is praying over the meal, but he keeps praying to "Baby Jesus." His wife and father-in-law rebuke him, noting that Jesus eventually grew into a man. Ricky fires back and says he likes "the Christmas Jesus best." His wife responds by saying, "I want you to do this grace good, so that God will let us win [the race] tomorrow." His sons pipe up and say that they like to imagine Jesus as a ninja. And his best friend Cal says that he likes to picture Jesus in a tuxedo t-shirt, because it's like Jesus is saying, "I want to be formal, but I'm here to party." Cal adds, "I like to party, so I like my Jesus to party."

Each of these characters had created an inaccurate version of God. Ricky's wife viewed God as kind of a magic genie that existed to allow them to win races and get rich. The sons pictured Jesus as a ninja because little boys like ninjas. Cal worshiped a view of God that was tolerant of his sins. And Ricky preferred worshiping the baby version of Jesus instead of the adult God-Man because he would rather cuddle Jesus than bow to him as Lord.

As ridiculous as this movie and illustration is, it speaks volumes to me. While we may laugh at how silly these characters are in their views of God, we can be guilty of doing the same thing. We can worship an inaccurate version of God. Our view of God can either be taught to us or we could create it ourselves. How can this be true? There can be some generations or denominations that view God as very stiff, serious, and unapproachable. Emerging generations can view God as tolerant of sin or sinful lifestyles. Some even go as far as to believe that every religion worships the same God.

There was a time in my life where I worshiped a version of God I created in my image rather than worship the one in whose image I was made. In my mid-twenties I learned an ugly truth about myself. I learned that I had some anger issues. I wasn't violent, but I did have some repressed anger from my childhood and my cynical nature, and I harbored bitterness and resentment because of some toxic church environments that I had witnessed at certain periods of my life growing up. Because I was an angry soul, I viewed God as a perpetually angry God. My god demonstrated very little grace, mercy, and patience. Though I wouldn't describe him in this way, it was clear that I believed these things about Him. I wasn't extreme like the Westboro Baptist Church, but I didn't show much love, grace, or patience to those who didn't think the same way I did. That way of living was exhausting. That god was life draining. Thankfully, the Lord revealed this sin to me and has been doing his good work of sanctification in my life ever since.

Many of us are living like the pagans Paul encountered in Athens. We worship an idol of "the unknown god" (Acts 17:23). That's what happens when we worship an inaccurate version of God. The real God is a stranger to us. We are living in idolatry, worshiping in ways that are forbidden.

God forbade us to make a carved image representing him because any image we make would be an inaccurate picture of

Him. He is the invisible God. He can't be contained or reduced to a mere man-made image, even if that "image" of God that we create isn't a physical idol.

God Determines Our Worship Practices

We don't call the shots in our worship practices. God is clearly the one who makes the rules and sets the standards. When Moses encountered God through the burning bush in Exodus 3, God said to him, "Do not come near; take your sandals off your feet, for the place on which you are standing is holy ground" (verse 5). Joshua was told something similar in Joshua 5:15.

God gave Moses two orders for this worship encounter: First, God told Moses not to come near. Second, he told Moses to remove his sandals. Why was Moses instructed in this way? Because that was "holy ground." We don't just go stumbling into God's presence any way that we want. God is holy and glorious and he is the King. Just like Moses, our interactions with God are not to be sloppy, careless, or casual.

It's worth noting that the removing of sandals at that time and place, was a custom of respect. Much like it used to be a custom for a man to remove his hat when he came into the building or was in the presence of a lady. It was a way of showing honor. When Moses encountered the Lord, God demanded this display of honor. He has every right to demand such a thing.

Can you imagine Moses responding with, "Nah. I think I'll keep my sandals on. That's just not the way I prefer to worship." I would question who or what Moses actually worshiped. If we think we are in charge of our worship practices and expressions, then it might not really be the Lord we are worshiping. We may be worshiping ourselves or our own preferences or traditions. True worship is an act of submission to our holy, righteous, and perfect Lord of all. It's a submission of joy, knowing that what he says is right and good.

Though we have been given much freedom in our New Testament worship practices, we don't have an "anything goes" approach. Whether or not our hearts are in the right place is not enough of a measuring stick. We must always use the Bible to guide, inform, and rule over our worship expressions. Bob Kauflin said it best: "Do what God clearly commands. Don't do what God clearly forbids. Use Scriptural wisdom for everything else."[14]

Discussion Questions

1. What are some ways that we can worship that are forbidden?
2. How do we worship God's way?
3. How can we worship an inaccurate version of God?
4. What beliefs about God have you had that you later learned weren't true?

Chapter 4
Worship God Reverently

G rowing up, I had a friend whose mom made us take off our shoes when we entered the house. I'm not necessarily advocating for that, because I don't have that rule at my own home, but it did cause me to have a much greater respect and reverence for their home. I was more careful and mindful about the things I did there. It reminds me again of when Moses encountered God through the burning bush and was instructed to take of his sandals out of an act of respect. This was not only symbolic of the fact that we don't just casually come stumbling into God's presence (as discussed in the previous chapter), but we are also to worship with honor and reverence.

The third commandment tells us, "You shall not take the name of the Lord your God in vain, for the Lord will not hold him guiltless who takes His name in vain" (Exodus 20:7). To "take" God's name denotes using it in speech. It can also be translated as "profess" or "lift up" the name of God. To take the name of the Lord means we are pledging our allegiance and loyalty to the Lord. This verse is specifically speaking of how we do that in worship.

Why is this the third commandment? The first two deal with worshiping only God, and doing it in a way that pleases

Him. We can go through the right motions, say all the right things, and still miss the point and fail to worship God like we should and like he deserves.

Vain Worship

If we were to read the Bible from cover to cover, we would only get a few chapters in before we saw the first of many examples of how the worship of God was taken lightly and done wrongly. It's within our broken nature to not worship God, so even as redeemed new creatures in Christ, as long as we wear this flesh, we will always battle the tendency to not worship God the way he demands and deserves.

We are told to not take his name in "vain." That word means "emptiness" or "worthlessness." King Solomon, the expert in all things "vain," warns worshipers of approaching God in a way that is empty and lacking in the reverence that he deserves: "Guard your steps when you go to the house of God. To draw near to listen is better than to offer the sacrifice of fools, for they do not know that they are doing evil. Be not rash with your mouth, nor let your heart be hasty to utter a word before God, for God is in heaven and you are on earth. Therefore, let your words be few" (Ecclesiastes 5:1–7).

So, how can we become guilty of taking God's name in vain as we worship? The first way is to use his name thoughtlessly. We are rightly offended when someone uses God's name as a curse word. That's blasphemy. But how often do we take God's name in vain during our worship practices? How often do we sing songs, recite Scripture, or pray prayers in a routine and careless way? When we speak God's name, does it carry significant weight every single time? If not, then it is being taken in vain.

Second, we take God's name in vain when we use it to pledge false loyalty. If on Sunday we are singing about how God is our everything and how we surrender all to him, but our lives Monday through Saturday don't reflect that at all, we are taking His name in vain. When we worship him on Sunday, it isn't out of weighty reverence because we leave the gathering completely unchanged and unphased.

Reverence for His Name

At some point during the Middle Ages, the divine name (Yahweh) was viewed as so holy that to speak it with unclean mouths such as ours would dishonor his holy name. During this time the Jewish authorities prohibited worshipers to even speak it. This is clearly an overreaction to people breaking the third commandment, but you have to appreciate the sentiment.

While God clearly doesn't forbid us from speaking his name, he does forbid us to do so flippantly. Rather, God's name is "glorious and awesome" and to be feared (Deuteronomy 28:58), exalted (Psalm 34:3), and blessed (Psalm 103:1) because his name is a strong tower (Proverbs 18:10) where there is life (John 20:31), and it is by no other name by which we are saved (Acts 4:12), and anyone who calls upon that name shall be saved (Romans 10:13). We are to hold fast to that name (Revelation 2:13) and do all things to his name (Colossians 3:17).

Our Lord Jesus provided for us the model prayer. He told us that when we pray, we should pray in this way: "Our Father in heaven, hallowed be your name. Your kingdom come, your will be done, on earth as it is in heaven" (Matthew 6:9–10). His template for our prayers begins with us acknowledging the holy and consecrated name of God our Father.

A popular genre in Christian literature today is heaven tourism, accounts from people who have "died," visited heaven, and then returned to tell the story . . . at an enormous profit. Besides the fact that Scripture tells us this would not be true (Proverbs 30:4; John 3:13), most of these claims of heavenly visitations differ greatly from the biblical examples of people who have had visions of heaven. Modern authors will describe their story of heaven with visits with deceased relatives and casual conversations with Jesus, the Holy Spirit, and even the devil. Scripture contains five examples of people who have had a vision of heaven (Isaiah 6; Daniel 7; Ezekiel 1; 2 Corinthians 12; and Revelation), and though they are brief, they are all consistent in their experiences: the overwhelming reverence of the glory and holiness of God.

Judgment on Irreverent Worship

The third commandment comes with a warning of judgment: "for the LORD will not hold him guiltless who takes His name in vain" (Exodus 20:7). This promise of judgment on taking God's name in vain is certainly not isolated. Leviticus tells us of an incident when a young man blasphemed God's name and God ordered the man, and any who would repeat that sin, to be put to death: "Bring out of the camp the one who cursed, and let all who heard him lay their hands on his head, and let all the congregation stone him. And speak to the people of Israel, saying, 'Whoever curses his God shall bear his sin. Whoever blasphemes the name of the Lord shall surely be put to death. And all the congregation shall stone him. The sojourner as well as the native, when he blasphemes the Name, shall be put to death'" (Leviticus 24:14–16).

Paul rebuked the Corinthian church for the abuse of the Lord's Supper in their worship gatherings. Partaking of Communion is a proclamation (1 Corinthians 11:26), and this had become a proclamation that the church was doing in vain. Paul rebukes them by saying, "Whoever, therefore, eats the bread or drinks the cup of the Lord in an unworthy manner will be guilty concerning the body and the blood of the Lord. Let a person examine himself, then, and so eat of the bread and drink of the cup. For anyone who eats and drinks without discerning the body eats and drinks judgement on himself. That is why many of you are weak and ill, and some have died" (1 Corinthians 11:27–30).

Fostering a Reverent Worship Culture

So, how do we as pastors, worship leaders, or church influencers foster a worship culture that is reverent and that takes God's name with holy honor when we worship? Here are three questions to ponder about your Sunday worship gatherings as well as your overall worship culture at your church.

The first question is: *How does your church use, speak, speak of, preach, and respond to God's Word?* This can be difficult, because every Christian church on the planet truly believes they are a Bible-based church that has a high view of Scripture. The truth is, you can throw a rock in any direction and it will land in the parking lot of a church where this is not reflected in their practices. A church has a high view of Scripture when it uses a lot of it in the service. They value Bible preaching when the Bible is the heartbeat of a sermon, not just a springboard. The church loves and values God's Word when they respond to it with repentance and praise. If we want to foster a worship culture that exalts and reveres God's holy name, we will only be able to do that with Scripture.

The second question is: *What is your ministry philosophy and approach on Sunday morning?* This is not a question of style, as there are strengths and weaknesses to every style of worship ministry. This is a question of content and overall goals. In other words, to create a worship culture of reverence for God's name, the content of your worship must be thoroughly Christ-centered (more on that later), with the supreme goal of lifting high the good name of our Lord. The Sunday morning goal for churches could be to appeal to outsiders and the lost, or to coddle the saints. But our primary focus, no matter our musical styles and preferences, should be to exalt God's name. As church influencers, it is your role to model and to teach your people to treasure that name above all else—above all of our preferences, comforts, and supposed needs.

Thirdly: *How do you describe and/or reference God?* There have been some fads in recent decades of having nicknames for God. Whether it's referencing Jesus as your "homeboy" or

God as "the Big Guy upstairs," I don't believe we are obeying the third commandment when we use cute monikers.

It would benefit all churches who are wanting to shape their worship culture to be more robustly biblical to do a study on the names of God. To learn and relearn the names of God that are revealed to us in Scripture eliminates the need to invent irreverent nicknames for him and leads us to take his name with honor and respect.

There have been many great names throughout history: George Washington, Martin Luther King Jr., Elvis Presley, Albert Einstein, etc. All of these names represent greatness in their place in history. I think of all of these names and more with great reverence and even awe. But the name of God is far greater. None of these names love you like he does. None of these names accomplished what Jesus's name has done. None of these names will last like Jesus's will last. Not one of those names will cause every knee to bow and every tongue confess Lordship. But Jesus's name will. No other name is worthy of all worship, adoration, and reverence.

Discussion Questions

1. Who are some people in your life and throughout history that you revere? Why?
2. What does reverence in worship look like?
3. What does irreverence in worship look like?
4. How can you foster reverence in worship?

Chapter 5
Worship God Consistently

God said to "Remember the Sabbath day, to keep it holy. Six days you shall labor, and do all your work, but the seventh day is a Sabbath to the LORD your God. On it you shall not do any work, you, or your son, or your daughter, your male servant, or your female servant, or your livestock, or the sojourner who is within your gates. For six days the LORD made heaven and e earth, the sea, and all that is in them, and rested on the seventh day. Therefore, the LORD blessed the Sabbath day and made it holy" (Exodus 20:8–11).

This commandment is unique from the other nine because it is the only one that is non-moral. It's also the only commandment that isn't clearly reiterated in the New Testament. It was meant to be a sign of the special relationship between God and Israel (Exodus 31:13–17). It's a gift from God to mankind in which we are to set aside one day in seven to rest from all of our labor, trusting in God's finished work of creation and redemption. We rest knowing that our eternity is secure and the fabric of the universe is being held together by Christ and not by our busyness.

The fourth commandment teaches us consistency. For the Jewish people, this was part of the rhythm of their lives. Every six days the Sabbath would begin on Friday at sundown and last until Saturday at sundown. Every week they would pause the busyness of their life and rest in the good work of God. They looked forward to focusing on the Lord, enjoying his good gifts, and refreshing their bodies, minds, and souls.

It's important for the modern Christian to have a good theology and practice of Sabbath. For us to do that, we must look at what the Old and New Testaments have to teach us about the Sabbath and consider what that looks like for us today as worshipers of God.

Sabbath in the Old Testament

God set for us the greatest example of observing the Sabbath when he instituted the practice after the six days of creation.

> Thus the heavens and the earth were finished, and all the host of them. And on the seventh day God finished his work that he had done, and he rested on the seventh day from all his work that he had done. So God blessed the seventh day and made it holy, because on it God rested from all his work that he had done in creation. (Genesis 2:1–3).

As a child, this always puzzled me. "Why would God need to rest? How could he get tired?" I thought. We know that an omnipotent and perfect God can't be drained of energy. That's not the reason God rested. He rested because he was finished. Notice the language in this passage: "The heavens and earth were finished . . . God finished the work he had done" (Genesis 1:1). God recognized that his work of creation was complete and "very good."

When we pause from our chaotic schedules, when we take a day of rest, we are certainly recharging our physical strength, because unlike God, we get tired. Deuteronomy 15:12 provides guidelines for a sabbatical year in which a servant will work for six years and on the seventh year go free. Leviticus 25:1–7 demands a sabbatical year of rest for the land. When we observe the Sabbath and when the Israelites observed the sabbatical year, we are doing more than just resting our bodies or the land. We are observing that the work was completed by God. He holds all of creation together without our help.

God takes this commandment (as he does the other nine) very seriously. In fact, he gave Israel a sobering consequence to anyone who would violate it: "These are the things that the LORD has commanded you to do. Six days work shall be done, but on the seventh day you shall have a Sabbath of solemn rest, holy to the LORD. Whoever does any work on it shall be put to death" (Exodus 35:1–2).

Numbers 15:32–36 records an incident where a man broke the Sabbath:

While the people of Israel were in the wilderness, they found a man gathering sticks on the Sabbath day. And those who found him gathering sticks brought him to Moses and Aaron and to all the congregation. They put him in custody, because it had not been made clear what should be done to him. And the LORD said to Moses, "The man shall be put to death; all the congregation shall stone him with stones outside the camp.: And all the congregation brought him outside the camp and stone him to death with stones, as the LORD commanded Moses."

Why did God give such a stern warning and follow through with having a man stoned to death? Theologians can cite various reasons, but at base it was an issue of idolatry. When we pause our lives, observe the Sabbath, and keep it holy, we are acknowledging that we are not God and that his work is perfect and complete.

Hebrew worshipers would gather on the Sabbath every week for worship. Traditionally, they would sing Psalm 92 every week. Note some of the lines from that Psalm: "For you, O LORD, have made me glad by *your work*; at the *works of your hands* I sing for joy. How great are *your works*, O LORD!" (verses 4–5, emphasis added).

The Sabbath offers a consistent beat for our lives in which we pause and reflect on the finished and perfect work of God. We find joy in it. And in it we find rest.

Jesus and the Sabbath

By the time we get to the New Testament, legalism was plaguing the practice of observing the Sabbath. Jewish tradition was held in higher esteem than God's own Word. The Talmud contained many outrageous rules and traditions that a Jew had to observe or, culturally speaking, be guilty of breaking the Sabbath.

These traditions wouldn't allow a person to travel more than three thousand feet to another person's house. Nothing could be bought or sold. No dishes or clothes could be washed. No letters were to be written. You couldn't pick grain or fruit to eat. No taking a bath or lighting a fire. You couldn't pick up any kind of tool or trade instrument, lest you be tempted to work.

You couldn't even carry anything heavier than a dried fig. You couldn't even toss something in the air and catch it because all of those things were considered "labor." As John MacArthur states, "The Sabbath was anything but a time of rest. It had become a time of oppressive frustration and anxiety."[15]

God gave mankind the Sabbath as a day of rest, but religious leaders twisted it into something that was completely opposite. Keeping up with all of the man-made rules, and worrying about being seen, judged, or even wrongfully executed made the Sabbath an exhausting and dreadful day.

Jesus challenged these false teachings of the religious establishment. One particular Sabbath day, Jesus said to the people: "Come to me, all who labor and are heavy laden, and I will give you rest. Take my yoke upon you, and learn from me, for I am gentle and lowly in heart, and you will find rest for your souls. For my yoke is easy and my burden is light" (Matthew 11:28–30).

It is ironic that Jesus said this for a number of reasons. First, it was on the Sabbath day, the day of rest. Second, he said it to an exhausted people who had a weekly day of rest built into their worldview and way of life. And third, because he was about to be accused by the religious establishment of violating the Sabbath because he refused to observe their ridiculous rules.

On that day he was walking through a grain field with the disciples. Being hungry, they plucked some grain to eat. Some Pharisees saw them and said, "Look, your disciples are doing what is not lawful to do on the Sabbath" (Matthew 12:2). Of course, it was unlawful according to them but not according to God.

Jesus responded by saying, "Have you not read what David did when he was hungry, and those who were with him: how he entered the house of God and ate the bread of the Presence, which it was not lawful for him to eat nor for those who were with him, but only for the priests?" (Matthew 12:3–4).

Here Christ is referencing 1 Samuel 21. In Jesus's day David was revered as a hero among the people, adultery and murder notwithstanding. Jesus points out that David himself ate on the Sabbath. And he didn't simply eat, but he ate bread reserved for the priests!

He goes on to say, "Or have you not read in the Law how on the Sabbath the priests in the temple profane the Sabbath and are guiltless? I tell you, something is greater than the temple here. And if you know what this means, 'I desire mercy, and not sacrifice,' you would not have condemned the guiltless. For the Son of Man is lord of the Sabbath" (Matthew 12:5–8).

Jesus recognizes that priests break the Sabbath every week but are excused so they can perform their priestly duties. Even though priests worked twice as hard on that day (something every minister can relate to), the legalistic Jews still didn't consider them breaking the Sabbath. In the same way, most Christians today don't consider teaching Sunday school, preaching, leading worship, or any other "ministry" activities as breaking the Sabbath. Jesus's use of the example of David and the priests lay bare the inconsistencies and logical flaws in the Pharisees' teachings on the Sabbath.

Sometime later Jesus was teaching in the synagogue on the Sabbath, and a man with a withered hand showed up (Luke 6:6). The Pharisees anxiously observed how Jesus would react to this man's affliction. If he did nothing, they could accuse him of not healing a man in need. If he did heal the man, they could accuse Jesus of working on the Sabbath. Jesus responds to them by saying, "I ask you, is it lawful on the Sabbath to do good or to do harm, to save life or to destroy it?" (Luke 6:9).

When Jesus healed the man, "the Pharisees went out and conspired against him, how to destroy him" (Matthew 12:14). Because the Old Testament law demands that "Whoever does any work on [the Sabbath] shall be put to death" (Exodus 35:2), they knew that could be their ticket to silence Jesus. They were not motivated by reverent desire to comply with Scripture. Jesus had bruised their egos. They were the religious elite. They were the most educated theologians, and this poor homeless man, who in their minds had been born out of wedlock, with misfit disciples, had just put them to shame in front of everyone.

Their motives weren't to honor God. It was about power and control. Their legalistic view of the Sabbath robbed it of its blessing. Jesus said, "The Sabbath was made for man, not man for the Sabbath" (Mark 2:27). God's people were never meant to be slaves of the Sabbath. It was meant to be a gift, not a burden.

The Sabbath for Today

The early church gathered together frequently. They were together at the ascension of Christ (Acts 1:6). Then, they traveled a day's journey into Jerusalem where they gathered together in the upper room (Acts 1:12–13). On the day of Pentecost they were together when they were filled with the Holy Spirit (Acts 2:1–4). Acts 2:42-47 provides us a blueprint for early church worship gatherings. It notes that they were committed to the fellowship (verse 42). It notes also that "all who believed *were together* and had all things in common" (verse 44, emphasis added). Verse 46 (emphasis added) notes that "*day by day*, [they were] attending the temple **together** and breaking bread in their homes."

So, is the command to remember the Sabbath and worship on Saturday still applicable to us as New Testament believers? Is it okay that we observe the Sabbath on a different day? Most early believers were Jewish. So, on Saturday they would worship and observe a traditional Sabbath worship gathering. But on Sunday they began worshiping in honor of the day on which the Lord Jesus had risen from the dead. As Christianity spread throughout the gentile world, the church was growing with large numbers of people that had no connections to Hebrew traditions and faith practices. Thus, the Sunday worship gathering became the norm for followers of Christ.

Neglecting Sabbath

Though most believers observe the Sabbath now on Sunday as "the Lord's Day," a consistent day of rest and worship has always been part of the Christian faith. It is still meant for us to pause our lives and rest in the finished work of God's creation, and now we also rest in the finished work of God's redemption through the cross (Ephesians 1:7). This is still meant to be a consistent beat in our lives. Our day of rest and worship is still to happen every seven days. Our bodies, our minds, and our souls need it.

Unfortunately, there is a growing trend and maybe even a spiritual epidemic of professing Christians neglecting this prescribed consistent rhythm in our lives. Twenty years ago, a person was considered an active church member if he went to Sunday services three or four weeks out of the month. Years before that, an active member was considered someone who attended every Sunday morning worship service, Sunday school, discipleship hour in the evening, followed by the Sunday night service, and a Wednesday night service. Now you are considered an active church member if you come only once or twice a month.

What soft and rebellious people we are! The early church faced persecution, torture, and death, yet they still gathered. They lacked resources, buildings, money, and sometimes even pastors. They had nothing to woo or attract people, yet they still assembled. Even today there are churches all over the world that still have to meet in secret. Many risk losing their families. Many risk being arrested. Many risk death. Yet they still gather.

The average American professing Christian neglects gathering with Christ's bride because he doesn't like the music, has to travel for ball games, had his feelings hurt, or maybe would just rather sleep in. Oh Christian, repent.

The writer of Hebrews 10:23–25 admonishes believers by saying, "Let us hold fast the confession of our hope without wavering, for he who promised is faithful. And let us consider how to stir one another up in love and good works, not neglecting to meet together, as is the habit of some." Do we really "hold fast the confession of our hope" when we are inconsistent in our weekly rest and worship? No. We are "wavering." For all of the petty excuses we may have for breaking the fourth commandment, it boils down to being an issue of spiritual warfare. The enemy doesn't want you to gather with believers. He doesn't want you to pause and rest in God's finished work of creation or Christ's finished work of redemption. He wants to rob God of this consistent beat of worship from you.

Here's some sobering reality: A Christian not faithfully connected to a local church is a foreign concept to the New Testament. It is quite possibly a symptom of an unconverted heart. Before I came to Christ, I hated *the* church and I hated *going* to church. One of the fruits of conversion that I see in my life is how God gave me a love for the church. It's difficult for me to see how a true, born-again Christian can have no affection for Christ's church.

If you claim to love Jesus, you will love the things he loves. And he not only loves but also gave himself up for the church (Ephesians 5:25). You can't really love me and not love my wife, so your claim of loving me would mean very little, if anything at all, if you had no regard for my bride.

The Sabbath and Our Burnout Culture

Full speed is the pace of life in today's American culture. There are many people who work full time during the day and nights and weekends at their side hustles. For those without evening jobs, life still doesn't seem to slow down. For those of us with kids, the regular routine of life is to come home from work, scarf down a quick dinner or grab some from a drive-through window as we rush off to take our kids to soccer practices, dance rehearsals, or music lessons, only to scramble to get the kids bathed, teeth brushed, and put to bed at something of a decent hour. When the weekend comes, many are traveling to the next ball tournament or catching up on yard work or laundry, only to start the whole process over again on Monday.

As a husband and a dad, I am always facing the tug between working more so that I can provide for my family as Scripture mandates and trying to slow down and foster the relationships I have in my home. Many spouses can relate to that. On top of being expected to work enough to meet financial needs, we are expected to spend time with our children, date our spouses, and have family worship times. And some churches bombard their congregants with expectations to be present at every event and involved in every activity or program.

Early on in my ministry I suffered through a season of severe burnout. My job description was three full pages of tiny font. Those duties consisted of being a youth pastor to a youth group with five different school districts represented, overseeing the music ministry, serving as the chaplain to the church's Christian school, and teaching two music classes per day. I also had associate pastor duties as well as any kind of outreach, assimilation, and benevolence duties that landed on my desk. All of that with the concluding clause: "and other duties as assigned."

When I began that ministry season, I was a fresh-faced newlywed. When I finished I was a father of two babies who had nothing of myself left to give to them. Because of unrealistic ministry demands, it came to a point where I was expected to spend my lunch "breaks" at a different school every day, my weekends at youth group activities, and my week nights doing other ministry events and/or preparing Sunday school lessons on my own time.

Even if I wanted to, I couldn't take a day off. A turning point came for me when I realized that getting out of bed in the mornings was a daily fight, and honestly, if I had just dropped dead I would have been okay with it. I was literally sacrificing my family at the altar of ministry, and I was working myself into an early grave.

The commandment to take a day of rest is the only one that ministers are often *expected* to break and, sadly, even reprimanded for observing it.

Thankfully, through reevaluation of priorities and in a continual pattern of repentance, I'm in a much healthier pace of life now. Even though I'm juggling more responsibilities than ever before, I don't have an oppressive pressure to neglect a weekly day of rest. Nowadays I don't feel the need to go and do every single church event or have my hand in every ministry program.

This overly busy lifestyle of Christians should come as no surprise because pastors and clergy don't model a healthy pace of life for the people they lead. Many pastors are burning out, and we are burning our people out with all of the busyness. Twenty percent of all pastor resignations is due to ministry burnout.[16] In fact, pastors are notoriously bad at self-care. The typical minister relegates physical exercise, nutrition, and sleep to a much lower priority than the average worker.[17] David Murray said, "God has given us instructions about how to live as his creatures, as the finite body-and-soul beings he has made us to be. But some of us are trying to live as if we are infinite. It's hardly surprising that we are breaking down."[18]

In church life, there is what's known as "the 80/20 rule." This means that 80 percent of the ministry work in the church is being done by only 20 percent of the people. Things are this way partially because of the large number of uncommitted Christians. A small minority of people are doing a large majority of the work also because they know that if the few don't step up, many things won't get done. I believe this to be largely true, but I don't believe that we should be burning out these faithful servants. I don't think we pastor them well when we teach them to neglect a consistent day of rest. If the 80/20 rule is true in your church because things simply wouldn't get done without it, may I suggest that you just allow things to not get done. Maybe many programs or activities that we do aren't really accomplishing anything for the kingdom. Or maybe we are trying to do so many things, we don't really do *anything* with excellence. We are spreading good people too thin.

The truth is, those of us who like to busy ourselves are just like the Pharisees. While they abused the Sabbath by inventing a multitude of restrictions on activities that you can't do on the Sabbath day, we abuse the commandment just in the opposite way. Instead of not allowing people to pick a fruit or grain to eat because it looks too much like working on the Sabbath, we work our people to death so that they *can't* observe a Sabbath rest. I once heard a pastor say, "If you are too busy to take a Sabbath, then you are too busy."

Our pattern of neglecting the Sabbath really boils down to reverting back to paganism. Deep down in our flesh, we believe that if we do something to appease our "gods," then we get results rather than resting in the security of what God has already done in his sovereignty. David Murray also said, "Lots of people call God *Creator* but live like evolutionists. It's as if life is about the survival of the fittest rather than about living like a dependent creature—trusting our Creator rather than ourselves—and according to our Maker's instructions."[19]

We are not meant to be slaves to the Sabbath. It wasn't given to us to oppress us. It was given to us so that we could be liberated. Our bodies, minds, and souls need a consistent beat of rest and worship.

Discussion Questions

1. What would you say constitutes a Christian being considered a regular attender of worship gatherings?
2. What are some of the reasons that frequency of church attendance has declined?
3. Why are most of us so bad at resting and observing a Sabbath?
4. What are some things that need to change in your life to make this a more frequent part of your week?

Chapter 6
A Balance of Spirit and Truth

One of the greatest passages of the Bible that helps to shape our theology of worship comes from the fourth chapter of John. Perhaps you are familiar with the story. It describes a day when Jesus and his disciples were traveling through Samaria, and Jesus stops to rest at a well while he sends the disciples into town, possibly to pick up some supplies. It is during the hottest part of the day (John 4:6), and a woman soon joins him to collect her water for the day.

There are some significant things going on before the theological discussion between the two begins. First, Jews were traveling through Samaria. This is something that wouldn't have happened. The Jewish people despised the Samaritans because centuries before, when the Jews were captured by the Assyrians, many intermarried with the pagan people and adopted their religious beliefs and practices. Those people settled in Samaria. When the Jews were freed and returned to their homeland, they found these impure, pagan people living on part of their land. The Samaritans were so despised by the Jews that they would have never spoken to one, much less traveled through Samaria, even if that meant they had to travel miles out of the way just to get to their desired destination.

Second, this woman disgraced her own people. As Jesus pointed out, she has had multiple husbands and is currently living with a man she is not married to (John 4:18). This sinful lifestyle was even looked down upon from her own pagan people, which is why she collected her water at the hottest part of the day. By going to the well at this time of day, rather than when it was cooler, she was able to avoid the other women of the town who would show up at the same time and converse with one another before beginning their day's tasks. A male Jewish rabbi would have never spoken to such a woman, much less ask her for a drink.

Third, this woman is curious and receptive to spiritual conversation. Jesus offers her the living water of eternal life (verses 13–14), which she is interested in receiving (verse 15). She recognizes that Jesus is a prophet (verse 19), though she doesn't yet know that he is *the* prophet whom Moses promised (Deuteronomy 18:15–19). And she wants to discuss the differences in worship practices between her people and the Jewish people.

Theological Question

This woman was able to discern that there was something different about Jesus. The ways this Jewish rabbi behaved so differently from the others and that he noted her lifestyle choices even though they had never met fanned the flames of her spiritual curiosity. She wanted to know more. She wanted to further discuss and discover what it means to truly be a child of God. So, she responds to Jesus by saying, "Sir, I perceive that you are a prophet. Our fathers worshiped on this mountain, but you say that in Jerusalem is the place where people ought to worship" (verses 19–20).

The woman posed a question about the location of worship. She knew that the Jews worshiped in Jerusalem according to Old Testament theology (2 Chronicles 7:12–16; Psalms 48:1–2; 132:13; Joel 3:17). Her people rejected most of the Old Testament Scriptures save the Pentateuch (first five books), so their theology was significantly underdeveloped, in particular their understanding of the geographical location of worship. The mountain she refers to in her question is Mount Gerizim. It was the place where Abraham took Isaac to be offered as a sacrifice (Genesis 22) and where Moses charged the tribes of Simeon, Levi, Judah, Issachar, Joseph, and Benjamin to bless the people of Israel after they cross over the Jordan River (Deuteronomy 27:11–12). So the mountain no doubt had special significance, but if she and her people would have kept reading through the Bible, they would have understood that God desired and demanded to be worshiped in Jerusalem.

In order to better understand the significance of her question about true worship, it is important to note the contrast of the two people groups that were represented here with the woman and Jesus and the cultures from which they came. As I previously stated, the Jews had the complete Scriptures. They were well versed in the Bible. They were orthodox in their theology, but their worship could be described as "cold" or "dead." They had the truth, but not much spirit or enthusiasm. In Mark 7:6 Jesus would say of his people: "This people honors me with their lips, but their heart is far from me; in vain do they worship me."

The Samaritans, on the other hand, only embraced part of God's Word and also implemented pagan doctrines and practices into their religious system. They were not only uninformed, but they were also misinformed as it related to sound doctrine. But their worship gatherings would pass as "lively" and "energetic." Their worship expressions were full of spirit, but they were starving of the truth. Their worship life could be described as what John MacArthur calls, "enthusiastic heresy."[20]

The extremes that these two cultures represented still exist today. For some people and/or churches, worship practices are very spirited, energetic, and passionate. They are physically and emotionally expressive, as God intended. But perhaps they are lacking in a solid understanding of what worship actually is. Maybe they can't fully or correctly articulate what the gospel is, or they may have an underdeveloped theology of the attributes of God. They probably have even adopted some worship practices that are forbidden in Scripture.

Other people or churches may seek to be faithful to the Scriptures in every element of their worship gatherings. They preach sound doctrine, dedicate significant portions of their worship service to Scripture readings, and their songs are based on God's Word. But perhaps they are emotionless. Emotions may even be suppressed and expressiveness discouraged. They love God and his Word, but you may not be able to tell it based on their facial expressions and body language.

It's these kinds of extremes that Jesus and the woman came from and it is what Jesus taught us that we must all try to avoid.

Jesus's Response

In response to the woman's question about the *where* of true worship, Jesus explains the *what* of true worship: "Woman, believe me, the hour is coming when neither on this mountain nor in Jerusalem will you worship the Father. You worship what you do not know; we worship what we know, for salvation is from the Jews. But the hour is coming, and is now here, when the true worshipers will worship the Father in spirit and truth, for the Father is seeking such people to worship Him. God is spirit, and those who worship him must worship in spirit and truth" (John 4:21–24)."

What does this mean? What does it mean to worship "in spirit and truth?"

Worship in Spirit

To worship in spirit is not referring to the Holy Spirit, though we certainly do that. In this particular context, Jesus is referring to the human spirit. It includes expressing praise physically, emotionally, and audibly with passion and sincerity.

Every church that I know of, whether they be cold and dead or vibrant and lively, sings in their worship gatherings. Scripture commands us over one hundred times to sing. Why is this? There are many reasons, but for the sake of this discussion, one of the primary reasons is because music is meant to stir within us an emotional response. It is meant to be accompanied with passion. Some other biblical expressions of spirited worship include raising hands (Psalm 134:2), clapping hands

(Psalm 47:1), dancing (2 Samuel 6:14), bowing down (Psalm 95:6), and shouting for joy (Psalm 47:1)—just to name a few.

I've heard people—even respected Bible scholars—refer to these practices as "charismatic stuff." I get flabbergasted every time. Those expressions aren't charismatic . . . they're biblical! I've had many people on worship teams that I've led over the years come to me privately and ask if it would be okay if they raise their hands in worship while they are on stage. Every one of them, in humility, would state that it's because they wouldn't want to offend anyone. My response would always be: "If someone comes to me asking why you are raising your hands, I'll ask them why they aren't."

There's some seriously unhealthy cultural flaws that many have grown up in, be it men who teach their sons to suppress their emotions, or churches that discourage expressiveness. If a Christian's excuse for not being expressive and spirited in worship gatherings how they were raised, their cultural up-bringing, or their denominational practices, then those things are wrong and must be repented of.

Rory Noland states:

It is simply unnatural to restrain our worship. It's human na-ture to exude joy and energy. We get visibly exercised over a new car, a good meal, or our favorite movie. When discussing sports, religion, or politics, many of us are very animated; we use our hands to emphasize certain words or phrases. When we speak about a loved one, our eyes light up, we smile; our feet may even bounce as if they're about to break into dance. I don't know anyone who speaks in constant monotone, with no facial expression, hands glued to their sides when talking about something or someone they love. Yet that's how some of us try to worship. Meanwhile the saints in heaven are do-ing face plants in homage to the King of kings.[21]

For far too long churches and individual believers have held onto this crutch in order to excuse their half-hearted worship offering. We would be hard-pressed to find believers in this country who would give the same unenthusiastic praise to their favorite sports team or if they were asked to stand and sing the "National Anthem."

The Bible has much to say about passionless worship. Christians who find themselves in this kind of practice must repent. Christian leaders must teach what healthy, spirited worship looks like. They must teach from the Bible and they must teach by example.

Worship in Truth

Leadership can only encourage spirited worship. They can teach it, model it, and even try to foster an environment for it. But, they can't control or manufacture it. They can, however, control whether or not a church is worshiping in truth. If they are faithful in that area, and they do what they can to encour-age and model spirited worship, then they will be prepared to create a healthy, balanced worship culture. Remember, pastor or worship leader, you are called to make good theologians. Teaching is part of the Great Commission, and the way that we lead in worship will teach the worshipers about the gospel of Christ, the character of God, and the function of his church.

So, what does this look like? When a church worships in truth, what are some characteristics that one might find present in that local congregation? First, the most blanket statement that I can make on this is that the content of our worship should be Christ-centered. I will expound upon this in the next chapter, but for now I will just say that all things should be to and about God and His only begotten Son.

Second, our worship should be guided by the Scriptures. Trends and practices in Christian worship come and go. Some have been good, some bad, and some indifferent. The most important thing that we must remember is that our worship practices must primarily come from what is found in Scripture. It doesn't mean that we don't have freedom to do things that are not necessarily in the Bible (though we should never do things that are clearly forbidden). But this means that what guides your church's worship culture shouldn't be the secular culture, what's hip, or even what your church has traditionally done. Scripture is our authority in all things, especially in our worship.

Third, our worship gatherings should be filled with the Scriptures. The most important words that will be spoken, prayed, or sang are not the words of the pastor, worship leader, or the congregation. The most important words will be the words of our God. This means that our worship gatherings should be pregnant with and full of the Bible. Our songs should be based on Scripture. It would be even better if our songs are Scriptures set to singable melodies. There should be Scripture readings. If you have screens, as most churches do now, project God's Word during preludes and instrumental breaks. When we pray, our prayers shouldn't be jumbled ramblings. How great and reverent would it be if we pray God's Words back to him?

The most obvious ways that our worship gatherings can be filled with the Scriptures is through preaching, as that typically takes up the majority of time in Christian worship gatherings. Entire books can and have been written on this subject, but I will just say that preachers must be faithful to the Word when they stand before their congregations. The church today doesn't need to be given baby food. They need the meat of the Word. For far too long the gospel has been dumbed down to where it's not even the gospel anymore. Pastors, when you stand before Christ's sheep, feed them. Your calling and responsibility is not to give them a soft message or a motivational speech. Your responsibility is to lead them to worship God Almighty in the truth of his perfect Word.

Every church, every follower of Jesus, every reader of this book should honestly evaluate themselves concerning their faithfulness to the Word. Because here's the deal: Everyone thinks they are doing it right. Every preacher believes they are accurately preaching the truth, when many are not. Every church believes that they are functioning the scriptural way, even though churches contradict one another in their practices. We all fall short. We all are imperfect creatures with vast room for improvement. We will never grow in our faithfulness to worship in truth if we choose to stay blind to our imperfections. We must ask ourselves hard questions. About everything you do in your church, ask yourself: Why do we do this? When did we start doing this? Are we worshiping in truth when we do this?

We should evaluate worship practices like our song lyrics, preaching methods, how and when we partake of Communion, how we pray, and how we give, just to name a few. We must seriously reevaluate other things that Scripture does not prescribe, such as announcements, the "stand and greet" time, patriotic symbols or services, Mother's Day services, and graduate Sunday.

Jesus Calls for a Balance

The Jews and the Samaritans represented an imbalance of worship practices. People today are no different. While both spirit and truth must be present for true worship to happen, I have found that, most of the time, Christians individually and churches collectively will do one or the other very well. We are all prone to imbalance. We will all naturally gravitate toward one and be weaker in the other. There are several contributing factors to this. One is of our theological or denominational background. Some come from a more expressive and free-flowing worship culture while others come from a very structured and liturgical background. Another contributing factor is our own personality. Some are naturally more expressive and others are more reserved and contemplative. A third contributing factor is our own up-bringing and life experiences. Many of us learn to worship from our parents and the worship settings that they place us in. None of these things are bad, but we must be aware of their reality as we seek to grow into the worshipers that God desires us to be.

Our call, if we want to be true worshipers of God, is to strive for a balance of both. This will take spiritual discipline, sanctification, and, in some cases, even repentance. But take heart. God is with you in this journey and he is for you and your sanctification. He offers grace and patience with us as we seek to grow into better worshipers of Him. He delights in your acknowledgement of your own weaknesses, and he guides you in this area of sanctification.

Discussion Questions

1. What are some ways that we worship in spirit?
2. What are some ways that we worship in truth?
3. Would you say your worship is more in spirit or truth?
4. How are some ways that you can grow in the area that is weaker in your life?
5. Would you say your church is more on the spirited side or more on the truth side?
6. How can you encourage the stronger and grow in the weaker?

Chapter 7
Christ-Centered Worship

I t seems redundant, but is still necessary to say: Christian worship must be centered on Christ. If our worship gatherings aren't centered on Jesus, then what's the point? If God is not the focal point of our worship, then it is idolatry.

These statements may seem painfully obvious, because they are. But the reality is, every believer will have a tendency to drift away from Christ-centered worship. Because of this, it is something that we must guard, fight for, and pursue with all of our might. Church leaders must be willing to face criticism for it. Church members must be willing to hold their church leaders accountable to it. It's that important.

If our worship is not Christ-centered, then who or what are we really worshiping?

Christ-Centered Worship in the Old Testament

To understand what Christ-centered worship looks like, we don't begin with the New Testament but with the Old Testament. Even thousands of years before Jesus was born in Bethlehem, the worship practices of God's people were centered on the person and future work of Jesus Christ.

Offering and Sacrifices

The first seven chapters of Leviticus outline the different types of worship offerings that the Isrealites were required to practice and observe. They were given instructions on grain offerings (chapter 2), peace offerings (chapter 3), sin offerings (chapters 4–5), guilt offerings (5:14–6:7), and priestly instructions (6:8–7:38).

Leviticus 1 provides instructions for the burnt offerings. The animal must be a male without blemish (verse 3), meaning that he was the best and most valuable of the herd. In fact, Numbers 18:17 more specifically requires that the animal be the "firstborn," just as Jesus is "the firstborn of all creation" (Colossians 1:15) and "the firstborn from the dead" (Colossians 1:18). Of course, this points to our Savior, who was a male and without the blemish of sin. The worshiper would place his hand on the head of the animal (Leviticus 1:4), symbolically identifying with the animal. The animal would be killed and the blood spilled (verse 5), and when they would cut it into pieces (verse 6) it would be burned and would be a "pleasing aroma to the Lord" (verses 9, 13, 17). This imagery is applied to Christ as Paul notes in Ephesians 5:2 that he "gave Himself up for us, a fragrant offering and sacrifice to God.

The Temple and Tabernacle Furnishings

The Old Testament prescribed in great detail the furnishings of the tabernacle, and later the temple. There is good reason for this. Each piece existed to symbolically communicate something. Many of those elements existed to point to the coming Messiah.

The Lampstand
As you entered through the doors of the holy place, the table of showbread was to the right and the lampstand was to the left. It functioned as the source of light for the tabernacle. In John 8:12 Jesus said, "I am the light of the world."

Exodus 25:31–40 gave explicit instructions on the construction of the lampstand. It was to be made of pure gold (verse 31), symbolizing Jesus's deity. The gold was specifically to be hammered into shape, not molded (verse 31), because Jesus was to be beaten as he would be prepared for crucifixion. The cups were to be shaped like almond blossoms (verse 33). The almond tree was the first tree to blossom in the Spring. This was to represent firstfruits and new life. New life, that we as Christians know, is provided by Christ.

The Altar of Incense
Exodus 30:1–11 describes the construction of the altar of incense. It was a foursquare box that made of acacia wood (verse 1) and covered in gold (verse 3). Again, gold represents Christ's deity, and the wood represents his humanity. Once a year a blood sacrifice was put onto the horns of the altar (verse 10).

Twice a day (morning and evening) the priests would burn incense on the altar (verses 7–8). The incense symbolically represented the prayers of the people rising up to heaven. In fact, God said that he would meet with them in this place (verse 6). It was there God would speak to his people. In fact, this is where Gabriel met with Zachariah to tell him about the birth of his son, John (Luke 1:5–20). This was important because it's through Jesus, the God-Man, that we are able to pray to and commune with God the Father.

The Table of the Bread of Presence

The bread of presence, also known as the table of the showbread, was prescribed in Exodus 25:23–30. God wanted a table of bread to always be in the temple in order to symbolize the meal of covenant fellowship that Israel enjoyed with the Lord. Just as friends and family share a meal together because of their shared love for one another, the bread of presence was to demonstrate a fellowship and love that God and his people enjoyed together.

In John 6:35 Jesus refers to Himself as the "Bread of Life." He used this familiar imagery to communicate that fellowship between God and mankind would be provided through him and his eventual broken body. Because the "Bread of Life" was broken on our behalf, we can now "break bread" with our Heavenly Father.

The Ark of the Covenant

The ark was to be constructed with acacia wood (Exodus 25:10) and covered in gold (verse 11). This to represent Christ's sinless humanity (wood) and his deity (gold). It was made with rings and poles for carrying (verses 11–15) by the priests. God knew his worshipers would be traveling and that it would be many years before the ark would have a home. Also, no one was to lay hands on the ark because it was disrespectful to God for sinful hands to touch the ark (2 Samuel 6:5–7).

The ark contained Aaron's rod (which had budded), a jar of manna from the desert, and the tablets of God's law (Hebrews 9:4). These were symbols of God's deliverance. They represent three aspects of Christ's life. The budded rod indicates that life can come from death. Just as the dead rod blossomed again; Jesus would one day bloom from his grave. The manna was God's provision of food for Israel while in the wilderness; Jesus was God's provision of Christ, the "Bread of Life." The manna gave Israel physical life, and Jesus gives us eternal life. The tablets of God's law were the character and requirements of God's holiness, which were fulfilled in Jesus (Matthew 5:17).

On top of the lid sat the "mercy seat." (verses 16–21) Once a year, on the Day of Atonement, the high priest would enter the most holy place to appear before the Lord (Leviticus 16:34). He would sprinkle the blood from the sacrifice onto the ark (Leviticus 16:14). This was to be a picture of Christ's blood allowing us to approach God (Hebrews 9:12).

The ark is where God would meet with the priest (Exodus 25:22). We cannot escape God's presence (Psalm 139:7–8), but there are varying degrees of his manifest. Here at the ark God was not demonstrating the full force of his glory. He was just giving a small degree of it, just enough for the priests to be able to handle it but also enough for them to know that God was sovereign.

It's much like when I wrestle with my kids. I don't wrestle with them with my full strength. When I pin them, I don't put my full weight on them. But I act with just enough intensity that they can endure while also imposing my will and strength upon them so that they know . . . I'm the man.

The ark was utilized by God to show a glimpse of himself in his glory. This revelation was to stir a response of worship as it foreshadows the coming Messiah, the one who will rule and reign and cannot be defeated.

The Feasts

Leviticus 23 details the feasts that the Hebrew people regularly observed. What Old Testament believers didn't know was that this calendar of events was an outline for the future work of Christ.

The Sabbath (verses 1–3)
Sabbath happened every single week. It was a special sign between God and his covenant people. It was a time for them to pause from all of life's demands and rest in God's finished work of creation. For new covenant believers we rest not only in God's finished work of Creation, but we rest in Christ's finished work of redemption.

The Passover (verses 4–5)
Exodus 12 records the first Passover. It was the night of the tenth and final plague when death would pass through Egypt, killing the firstborn of every household. God made covenant with his people in that they were to kill a lamb "without blemish" (Exodus 12:5) and put its blood over the doorposts of their house (verse 7). God promised: "This shall be a sign for you on the houses where you are. And when I see the blood, I will pass

over you, and no plague will befall you to destroy you, when I strike the land of Egypt" (verse 13). He goes on to say, "For the LORD will pass through to strike the Egyptians, and when He sees the blood on the lintel and on the two doorposts, the LORD will pass over the door and will not allow the destroyer to enter your houses to strike you. (verse 23).

Every year, from that night onward, the Jewish people would celebrate the Passover with a meal. Each element of that meal was full of symbolism. There were six elements of the Seder meal, but the most important one was the *Z'roa*, which was a roasted lamb bone. This was not to be eaten; it was simply to remain on the table as a reminder of the lamb that was slain for each house on the night of the first Passover. Christians have a more complete realization of the importance of that element. We, like the Jews, know that the slain lamb that night stopped death from overtaking God's people. But we also know that this pointed to something greater: the coming of the Perfect and spotless Lamb who would shed his blood to atone for our sins and would prevent us from suffering a spiritual death.

This annual worship practice was and still is centered on the person and work of Jesus.

The Feast of Unleavened Bread (verses 6–8)
For seven days the Hebrew people ate only unleavened bread with their meals. They were to cleanse all the yeast from their homes. In Scripture, leaven depicts sin (Luke 12:1; 1 Corinthians 5:6). The purpose of this feast was to remind God's people that they are called to be separated from sin. Jesus ultimately made this possible by cleansing believers from sin by salvation through his blood.

The Feasts of Firstfruits (verses 9–14)

This feast happened the day after the Sabbath that follows the Passover. The priest took the first sheaf of barley from a field and waved it as an offering before the Lord. This was to symbolize that the first and the best of everything belongs to God.

The New Testament offers further clarity on the meaning of this symbolism when it notes that Jesus is the firstfruits (1 Corinthians 15:20). In John 12:23–24 Jesus also compared his death and burial to the planting of a seed. Life from a buried seed comes up from the ground, just as Jesus came out of the grave alive after being buried.

The Feast of Weeks/Pentecost (verses 15–21)

Instead of waving sheaves before the Lord, like in the Feast of Firstfruits, the priest would wave two loaves of bread that were baked with leaven. These two loaves represented the Jews and the gentiles. This imagery was fulfilled in Acts 2 when the Christian church was born and the Holy Spirit came and united the Jewish and the gentile believers into one worshiping family of God that is united in their belief in Jesus as the Christ.

The Feast of Trumpets (verses 23–25)

This feast took place on the first day of the seventh month (September). For the Jews, this was the first day of a new year. Just like our celebration of a new year on the first of January, this day for them was about new beginnings and fresh opportunities. It was a day used for prayer and a time when God's people could refocus and recommit to the Lord.

Israel over time become a scattered people. Trumpets were used to gather them together. One day, God will gather all believers together with the sound of a great trumpet: "For the Lord Himself will descend from heaven with a cry of command, with the voice of an archangel, and with the sound of the trumpet of God. And the dead in Christ will rise first. Then we who are alive, who are left, will be caught up together with them in the clouds to meet the Lord in the air, and so we will always be with the Lord" (1 Thessalonians 4:16–17).

The Day of Atonement (verses 26–32)

This feast happened after Israel had been gathered together for the Feast of Trumpets. It was a time of rest, worship, and cleansing. As Christians, we know that God's scattered people will be gathered together in the last days and will enter into eternal cleansing, secure in the perfect and finished atonement of Christ.

The Feast of Booths (verses 33–44)

Also known as the Feast of Tabernacles, this was a time of reflection for when God's people were mobile. They lived in tents and booths. They worshiped in a temporary and transportable tabernacle. The Feast of Booths was meant for them to reflect on and celebrate God's faithfulness to them in the past.

It was a festival of gratitude, much like America's November holiday of Thanksgiving. It was a celebration of joy that can only be found in Christ.

Christ-Centered Worship: The Practice of Jesus

Jesus was the perfect man. In all of his ways he obeyed and glorified the Father without fail. He truly did all things "to the glory of God" (1 Corinthians 10:31). He showed what it means to be a worshiper, both in his teachings and by his example.

Jesus proclaimed to the Pharisees that all Scripture was about him: "You search the Scriptures because you think that in them you have eternal life; and it is they that bear witness about me" (John 5:39–40). From the beginning to the end of the Old Testament, we see the story of worship unfold. In Genesis 1 God shows us through his acts of creation that his name is to be praised when he declared his own acts "good." In Genesis 3 worship is broken when sin entered into the world through Adam's rebellion. Exodus and Leviticus prescribed detailed worship practices. The prophets admonished God's people for careless worship and idolatry. So, as we see worship threaded throughout every page of Scripture, and as Jesus said that all of Scripture is about him, we can easily conclude that all worship is to be centered on him because of his perfect nature and his good works.

Like any faithful Hebrew, Christ observed the annual Passover. On the night that he was betrayed and arrested, he and his disciples were observing the meal and it was there that Jesus instituted a staple of Christian worship practices known as the Lord's Supper. He made it very clear that this practice was centered on him as the Savior.

Luke 22:19–20 records: "And *He* took the bread, and when *He* had given thanks, He broke it and gave it to them, saying, 'This is *my* body, which is given for you. Do this in remembrance of *me*.' And likewise the cup after they had eaten, saying, 'This cup that is poured out for you is the new covenant in MY blood'" (emphasis added). He was explicitly showing them that the focus of worship was to be on no one else but the Savior.

After partaking of the first communion meal, Scripture says they sang a hymn (Mark 14:26). This was part of Jewish custom. Worshipers would commonly sing the *Hallel* (Psalms 113–118).

Jesus was fond of singing psalms. We can see that in his final moments on the cross his mind went to the Psalter. Matthew 27:46 and Mark 15:34 record him quoting Psalm 22:1: "My God, my God, why have you forsaken me?" Luke 23:46 notes him reciting Psalm 31:5: "Into your hand I commit my spirit." Jesus not only taught us about how to be worshipers, he himself modeled faithful worship. As he sung psalms of praise as a young boy in the temple, with his disciples in the upper room, and in his dying moments on the cross, he sung about Himself.

Christ-Centered Worship: The Practices of the Early Church

The first Christians carried on with the example given to them by the Old Testament and by the Lord himself during his earthly ministry.

Elements from Acts 2

We are given much freedom in how we worship the Lord today. Compared to the Old Testament, we don't have very many pre-scribed worship practices. Because of this, we must be faithful to observe the few elements that we are commanded to participate in. Acts 2:42 briefly describes early Christian worship gatherings: "And they devoted themselves to the apostles' teaching and the fellowship, to the breaking of bread and the prayers." This verse notes four primary elements of Christ-centered worship.

The first is the apostles' teaching. This included their teachings of the Godhead from the Old Testament, the law, the new covenant, etc., and their writings and instructions that were forming the New Testament. Modern-day worshipers we be devoted to the apostles' teachings when Gospel-centered sermons in which Jesus is the hero. We do this when we have intentional Scripture readings during our gatherings.

The second element of Christ-centered worship is when we are devoted to the fellowship. If we truly love Christ, we will love his bride. Being centered on Christ means that we are committed to other Christ-centered worshipers. The purpose of the fellowship is to build one another up in Christ so that we can become more and more Jesus-focused people.

The third element mentioned in Acts 2:42 was that the early believers were devoted to the breaking of bread. This is similar to the previous element because they usually happened together. The breaking of bread does not specifically mean partaking of communion. It is a general term of sharing a fellowship meal with one another. However, church history does provide clarity about fellowship in that the early Christians frequently observed the Lord's Supper. They often observed it several times a week. They would partake of communion following a fellowship meal together.

The fourth element of worship that the early church was devoted to was prayer. These prayers were focused, sincere, unhurried, and Christ exalting. They were a praying people. They were fully dependent on Christ. Culturally speaking, they were powerless. They didn't have prestigious jobs or political connections. They were hunted, persecuted, and martyred. This drove their worship gatherings to be an intensely prayerful pursuit of Christ.

Orderly Worship

The apostle Paul spends a large portion of his first letter to the Corinthian church addressing issues of immorality and their broken worship practices. It was so bad that he acknowledged in 1 Corinthians 11:17 that, "When you come together it is not for the better but for the worse." Their worship gatherings had become so chaotic and self-centered that there was no spiritual benefit to their existence as a church. That's a pretty weighty indictment on a worship gathering.

In Chapter 14 Paul admonishes the church for their misuse, abuse, and misunderstanding of the spiritual gifts of tongues and interpretation. He notes that, as far as our worship gatherings go, "All things should be done decently and in order" (1 Corinthians 14:40).

Charismatics are often accused of needing to pay attention to this verse. This makes sense, especially since Paul is speaking about the misuse of tongues. But what about the many denominations that don't practice or observe the gift of tongues? Are they exempt from this admonishment that "All things should be done decently and in order"?

There are many ways that a church can demonstrate unhealthy worship patterns through disorderly worship even if it is not of the charismatic persuasion. All of my life I have been in the Protestant faith. Something that I've learned about Protestants is that many can criticize charismatic believers for having disorderly worship while they often have their own version of disorderly worship. This is often the case when there is a lack of planning, organization, and communication. A general lack of excellence is often given a hall pass in many churches. I can't tell you how many worship gatherings I've been in where transitions between spots and general flow of a service are largely ignored. I have been in many worship services that are nothing short of disorganized, disorderly, and chaotic.

How is orderly worship Christ-centered? When our worship is not orderly, our flesh will cause distractions. If our gatherings are not orderly, they are not intentional. When we are not intentional, we become centered on other things. Our hearts are fickle and wayward. If we lack intentionality and order, our hearts *will* drift to our idols. And when this happens individually, it won't take long for it to happen collectively. If we want a healthy worship culture, we must be Christ-centered. If we want to be Christ-centered, we must be orderly.

Songs of Substance

God's worshipers have always been a singing people. The largest book in the Bible (the Psalms) is a collection of worship songs. There are over one hundred verses in the Bible that command God's people to sing. This is no different for New Testament believers.

Paul charges the Ephesian church to "be filled with the Spirit, addressing one another in psalms and hymns and spiritual songs, singing and making melody to the Lord with your heart" (Ephesians 5:18–19). He says something similar to the saints in Colossae: "Let the word of Christ dwell in you richly, teaching and admonishing one another in all wisdom, singing psalms and hymns and spiritual songs, with thankfulness in your hearts to God" (Colossians 3:16).

Note the charge from Colossians that, through singing of psalms, hymns, and spiritual songs, the word of Christ will "dwell in you richly." It's also worth noting that singing is a source of teaching and admonishment. Every church should ask of their song repertoire, "What do our songs say?" Another good question to ask: Based exclusively on the songs we sang this past month, what would our congregation know about Christ?

Healthy churches sing. They sing often. They sing passionately. They sing about great truths of the Person and Work of Jesus.

Christ-Centered Worship for Today

Every church truly believes that they are Christ-centered, gospel-focused, Bible-driven, and the like. In reality, not every church is. It is important for every believer and every church to take a brutally honest inventory of their worship. Just because you *think* you are Christ-centered and biblical doesn't mean that you actually are.

Now, that doesn't mean that there aren't good things about every church. But if we only focus on the areas where we *are* Christ-centered and ignore areas in which we are *not*, it's like saying, "I'm totally fine. I have *both* of my lungs." Meanwhile, we may be neglecting to do anything about the lung cancer that is being expressed by a shortness of breath.

A lack of Christ-centered worship in the early church was called out as idolatry. Today, we accommodate it, excuse it, preserve it, embrace it, and even fight for it, even if that means firing our pastors and leaders. We need to figure out which areas we need to adjust, or maybe even repent of. There are also some steps that I believe are necessary for our churches to possess a healthy worship culture by fostering Christ-centered worship.

Repent of Self-Centered Worship

The complete opposite of worship that is centered on Christ is worship that is centered on self. We are living in a day that seems more self-serving than ever. It's easy to blame this kind of behavior on Millennials or Generation Z, but the truth is, self-centeredness is not bound by any specific generation. It is a human-nature problem.

Today, our worship gatherings are being ruled by personality-driven leadership. In other words, the pastor or worship leader may be placed on a pedestal, and that is the foundation for which they lead and build their ministries. There is much to say about the entertainment-driven philosophy of worship gatherings. However, this consumeristic approach to worship has nothing to do with musical styles.

It's ironic. When we have iTunes and Spotify playlists, XM radio stations specifically for our preferred musical genres and artists, we are in complete control of any kind of music we consume, anytime and anywhere we want. You would think that it would be easier to surrender our musical preferences for twenty minutes of our week on a Sunday morning. Instead, our consumer-ruled culture has made it even harder for us to not be self-absorbed during worship.

Even much of the content of our worship is self-centered. For years, hymns like "Mansion Over the Hilltop" have been sung that make no reference to Jesus, only the trinkets he can give you. Songs like this and many found in the *Heavenly Highway Hymnal* make an idol out of heaven. Songs like that communicate that the goal is for a Christian to die and go to heaven so they can live like a king for all eternity, instead of the goal being to go to heaven to live with *the* King and worship him for all eternity.

Even the sermons we listen to can be more about how great we are rather than how great Christ is. How many times have you heard a sermon on David and Goliath? Has the point of application mostly been that you are like David and you have to slay the giants in your life? That's not the point of the story.

We are not David. The way we should look at that story is how Jesus has slayed our giant. Our giant, our unbeatable enemy—death—was conquered for us. And like David used Goliath's own weapon to finish him off, Christ used death's own weapon (the grave) to conquer it. We are not to be the hero of the story in any theologically correct sermon or song...Christ is.

Know the Value of Tradition and the Danger of Traditionalism

Tradition in and of itself is not bad. There are some worship traditions that are in place specifically because they honor God and center our hearts and minds on Jesus. Embracing good traditions can help us achieve worship that is truly Christ-centered. This happens when we use intentional liturgy. Even if you aren't from a high-church worship culture, every church has a liturgy of some sort. Consider using the Apostles' Creed or the Nicene Creed. Be careful not to reject time-tested practices because you deem them "traditional," because you may be falling into a new kind of traditionalism, one that rejects anything that isn't "new" or "cutting edge" or things that may seem too "Catholic."

Traditionalism is when we practice, observe, and guard traditions for the sake of tradition. *Tradition* is about honoring time-tested practices. Traditionalism is worship that is self-centered. Every established church has traditions but must fight against the temptation to traditionalistic idolatry.

Trade the Hallmark Calendar for the Liturgical Calendar

Another aspect of Christian tradition is the use of the liturgical calendar. Many worshipers reject the use of the liturgical calendar because, in their minds, it feels too close to what the Catholics do. But the truth is, the calendar is designed to keep our worship Christ-centered. We've traded the liturgical calendar for the Hallmark calendar. Instead of every service being themed around the gospel, we have services that center around Mother's Day, Father's Day, graduate Sunday, and patriotic holidays. It's a shame that we can have a more Christ-centered worship service at a Catholic Church (with which I have significant theological issues) on the Fourth of July than at a typical Baptist church.

Bryan Chapell said, "Christian worship is a re-presentation of the gospel. By our worship we extol, embrace, and share the story of the progress of the gospel in our lives."[22] Any worship practice that fails to accomplish this must be discarded. We must turn from things that aren't Jesus focused and cling to things that are. Worship is all about Christ, and anything else is idolatry, and sufficient study of Scripture will show us that idolatry reaps serious consequences.

Discussion Questions

1. What does it mean for our worship to be centered on Jesus?
2. What are some elements of worship that are Christ-centered?
3. What are some common practices in church that are not Christ-centered?
4. How can you tell when something is not Jesus-centered in our worship?
5. How does consumerism hinder Christ-centered worship?
6. What are the benefits of tradition and dangers of traditionalism?
7. What are some things in your church that must change in order to have a more Christ-centered worship culture?

Chapter 8
Committed to Communion

When compared to Old Testament worship, we don't have nearly as many prescriptions for our worship practices. The practice of communion (the Lord's Supper, the Eucharist, the Table, etc.) is one of the few elements of worship Scripture gives for new covenant believers, and it is one of only two ordinances of the church (the other being baptism).

Jesus instituted it on the night he was betrayed and arrested. This was one of the very last things that he taught his disciples. Acts 2:42 implies that this was one of the few practices that the early church "devoted" themselves to. Clearly, the partaking of the Lord's Supper is an extremely important element in Christian worship and should be made a priority, but it is often a rather misunderstood and neglected part of the liturgy in many churches.

Understanding Communion

Throughout church history, many doctrines and practices surrounding the Eucharist have developed. Some of them have been good, and some have not. There are many views on the nature of the Lord's Supper, but predominantly there have been three theological perspectives.

Transubstantiation

This doctrine began to develop in the ninth century, being taught by theologian Paschasius Radbertus. He taught that the elements of bread and wine transformed into the actual flesh and blood of Christ. This doctrine was declared part of the faith of the church in 1059. [23]

Consubstantiation

The Reformers combated the doctrine of transubstantiation, as it had very little support from Scripture and was more of a product of the mysticism of the time. Martin Luther developed the doctrine of consubstantiation, which taught that the elements don't physically transform into the flesh and blood of Christ,but that Christ is physically present during communion and that partakers are recipeients of his body. Luther took literally Christ's words: "This is my body."

Memorialism

This doctrine was championed by most Reformers, particularly Ulrich Zwingli. It is the belief that the elements were only symbolic in nature and that Christ was present, but he was *spiritually* present. This doctrine is the most consistent with Scripture and with most non-Catholic believers throughout Christian history. While transubstantiation and consubstantiation interpret Jesus's words as confirmation that the ele-

ments are his literal flesh and blood, we know that he was being symbolic and metaphorical because nowhere in Scripture
after Christ's resurrection does it imply that communion was
anything more than an act of memorialism.

How Do We Partake?

So, how is a New Testament believer supposed to partake of
the Eucharist? We aren't given a specific liturgical blueprint
for how this is to be done, but we should be mindful and intentional in in our method and manner of partaking.

Methods

There are many different ways that the believer partakes of
communion, depending on denomination or church tradition.
Each of these different methods communicate something significant in this act of worship. For example, you may come
from a tradition in which the clergy places the bread or wafer
directly into your mouth. This symbolizes that Christ's body
and blood, his sacrifice, was a gift that was *given* to you. Some
congregations break off a piece of bread, symbolizing Christ's
body being broken. Some dip the bread into the wine, demonstrating how Jesus's broken body was drenched in blood. Many
congregations allow participants to partake one at a time,
while many will wait until the elements are passed so that
the congregation can take them in unison, demonstrating the

church's unity in Christ. This same demonstration of unity is found when a congregation partakes of one cup.

Scripture doesn't prescribe a specific method. Most methods were developed by a particular philosophy and have been carried on through tradition. All of these methods are good, and so are many that are not mentioned. The important thing is that the chosen methods are intentional. Church leaders should use prayerful wisdom when deciding what method or methods they will lead their church to practice.

Manner

Though the methods of partaking of the Lord's Supper aren't prescribed in Scripture, the manner certainly is. Paul gave a sobering word of admonishment to the Corinthian church on partaking of communion in an unworthy manner: "Whoever, therefore, eats the bread or drinks the cup of the Lord in an unworthy manner will be guilty concerning the body and the blood of the Lord" (1 Corinthians 11:27).

How does one partake of communion in an unworthy manner? I believe there are three distinct ways (though there is overlap in these categories). The first way is by being unregenerate. The Lord's Supper is to be observed by those who have trusted in the work of Christ and have been redeemed by the broken body and spilled blood. The second way that we can partake in an unworthy manner is if there is disunity within the church. The Eucharist is to be celebrated by local congregations, and to partake together is to acknowledge your bond in Christ. If you partake of the elements while having active discord with a brother or sister, then you can be guilty of partaking in an unworthy manner. Finally, partaking unworthily is the result of unconfessed sin. This category certainly encompasses the previous two, but it is worth being distinguished on its own.

This unconfessed sin is the reason Paul charged the Christian to practice self-examination: "Let a person examine himself, then, and so eat of the bread and drink of the cup" (1 Corinthians 11:28). Just as church leaders should teach more on the practice of Communion, they should also teach more on self-examination. The worshiper should also be provided space within the worship service for self-examination, confession, and repentance before they partake of communion.

Failure to examine oneself, repent of sin, reconcile with one's brother, sister, and/or Savior while partaking of communion in an unworthy manner is a dangerous thing. Paul offers a sobering warning for those who do so: "For anyone who eats and drinks without discerning the body eats and drinks judgement on himself. That is why many of you are weak and ill, and some have died" (verses 29–30). How many Christians are in danger of facing judgment because they are partaking in an unworthy manner? I would dare say that they do so not out of full-on rebellion but because they are uninformed. This is why it is essential for this sacred act to be a priority in the church. It needs to be treated as sacred, observed frequently, and taught clearly in order for our churches to have a healthy worship culture and for individual worshipers to not be partaking under judgment but out of joy.

Frequency

How often are we supposed to partake? Scripture isn't explic-
ite on the frequency with which a church is to observe this
ordinance. Paul quotes Jesus as saying, "Do this, *as often as
you drink it*, in remembrance of me" (1 Corinthians 11:25). This
seems to imply that we are given freedom to observe communion as often or as little as we want, as long as we do it correctly, from a clear conscience, and from a worshipful heart.
But we must not base this philosophy on just one verse. We can
look to the practices of the early church.

Acts 2:46 states that, "*Day by day*, attending the temple together, and breaking *bread in their homes*, they received their
food with glad and generous hearts" (emphasis added). This implies that the first Christians met together every day, and part
of their daily worship practice was to partake of the Eucharist.
Sunday quickly became the day of worship for Christians. By
Acts 20, Sunday worship seems to have become normal practice for the church. Verse 7 notes, "On the first day of the week,
when we gathered together to break bread . . ." The Lord's Supper was held so sacred, and was such a priority for the church,
that they observed it every time they gathered to worship.

We can also use church history to guide us in our philosophy
of the frequency of observing this ordinance. Justin Martyr describes communion as occurring "on the day called Sunday."[24]
By the beginning of the second century (112 AD in Bithynia),
worship gatherings consisted of believers meeting together
early Sunday morning before work to sing, pray, and commit
themselves to holiness, then later in the evening after work to
sing, learn, share a meal, and partake of the Eucharist.[25]

The Lord's Table was central to the Christian worship service for centuries. Every element centered around, and built toward, its observance. Ken Duncan notes:

> After the ministry of the Word, the service began to direct its attention toward the Lord's Table. Non-baptized worshipers would first be dismissed, which left an assembly of the baptized faithful. These Christians then participated in the service's main intercessory prayers and actions, such as the exchange of peace.[26]

By the Middle Ages, sometime around the turn of the sixth century, major shifts began to happen within Christian worship. Worship practices began to be taken away from the people. The congregants began to become spectators rather than participants. Prayers were prayed, Scripture was read, and songs were sung not by the congregation but by the clergy.[27] The Lord's Table, which used to be central, not only in practice and emphasis but also physically central in the meeting place, was now being moved farther and farther from view until it was placed out of the way against a wall.[28] Because of this de-emphasis, observance of communion became less frequent.[29]

James White notes:

> the disinclination to receive from the chalice which became common in the twelfth century for fear of spilling the blood of Christ. Previously, people might drink through a straw or by dipping the bread in the chalice. For various reasons, most people ceased receiving communion frequently. Many devout people felt four times a year (Christmas, Easter, Pentecost,

and the patronal festival of their parish church) was sufficient and a whole series of councils and synods fussed at the popu-lace for neglecting to receive at least yearly at Easter.[30]

The philosophy of partaking of the Lord's Supper only four times a year originated from a philosophy of taking worship expressions and participation away from God's people. It came from the congregation being robbed of the joy and practice of congregational worship.

The Reformers did so much in leading the church back to truth. Not only did God use them to correct doctrines of so-teriology, ecclesiology, and bibliology, but they corrected the church's worship as well. They sought to bring worship ex-pressions and participation back to the people. For the first time in over a millennium, the church as a whole began to sing again, pray and hear God's Word in their own language, and participate in the Eucharist again.

One exception being the Swiss Reformer Ulrich Zwingli. Though we owe a great deal of gratitude for how God used Zwingli for good, he was definitely the least progressive of the Reformers as it pertains to most worship practices. Most Re-formers believed in the twofold structure of worship: Word and sacrament. Zwingli did not. His emphasis was only on preach-ing the Word. He believed that Scripture was the only thing the people should listen to. He abolished organs and other music. No pictures in the worship space or anything that he thought would detract from the centrality of the Word was allowed.[31]

Because of this singular emphasis on preaching, he con-tinued the medieval tradition of only having communion four times a year. His philosophy is influential among many Calvinists. Even staunch non-Calvinists are influenced by his lack of priority of this ordinance. This philosophy influenced the English Puritans, Baptists, Presbyterians, Congregationalists, and American Protestants. Communion, though it won't be openly admitted, is simply not as important in these circles. Where the Eucharist had been the central element in for centuries in Christian worship, the sermon was now central.

Another shift in emphasis happened beginning with the birth of Pentecostalism from the Azusa Street Revival of 1906 and again with the Jesus Movement of the late 1960s and early 1970s. Both of these movements were significant in ushering in the modern worship movement, which we are in today. The element of worship that is most emphasized in these traditions is not the Eucharist or the sermon but congregational singing.

While the Calvinists and the charismatics are arguing over whether the sermon or the singing should be longer, and while pastors want the sermon to be central and worship leaders want the emphasis to be musical, the Lord's Table is pushed aside, only to be brought out and dusted off a few times a year.

Many of the reasons that are given to justify such infrequent practice of communion are shallow. These include a desire to keep it special, to keep it from becoming routine, or it's simply the way they've always done it. The same kind of reasoning isn't given to any other element of worship. We don't see preaching, praying, singing, or especially *giving* only taking place four times a year in order to "keep it special." I would argue that we demonstrate that communion is not that special because of how infrequently we partake of it. I would argue that if we truly wanted it to be special, we would do it more often. With only four times a year, it would be easy for a believer to go all year long without celebrating the Lord's Table. And because of the infrequency of this element, the average Christian doesn't really understand the significance of the act. We don't have to reduce the amount of times we observe communion in order to "keep it special" because it already *is* special. It signifies the broken body and poured out blood of our Savior that purchased salvation for us. We need this visible and physical reminder of that good news every week.

The truth is, communion has become the red-headed stepchild of Christian worship. If we want to see our churches revitalized and our worship cultures thriving, we will have a renewed emphasis of this sacred worship expression.

Discussion Questions

1. How often did the early church partake of Communion together?
2. How often should present-day believers partake?
3. What are some ways that we can partake of the Lord's Supper in an unworthy manner?

Chapter 9
Committed to Excellence

We've all witnessed worship services that were disastrous, or at best sloppy and thrown together. I've known a musician to stop the flow of the musical worship and very loudly ask from across the stage what the next song was supposed to be and what key. I've seen carefully constructed worship services thrown out the window when the unprepared pastor or announcement guy comes up to fumble his way through his segment like he was Mr. Bean. And I've witnessed the all-too-common train wreck of a tone-deaf vocal solo.

We don't allow a lack of excellence in any other area of life. If we did that in our non-ministry jobs, we would be fired. If we did that in our marriages, it could lead to divorce. We certainly don't do it with our hobbies. So, why do we give a lack of excellence a pass when it comes to the worship of God? Why does the church give mediocrity a platform? Why do we tend to showcase a lack of quality? It is a mindset and philosophy that must be repented of because it is unbiblical.

Joyful Noise?

Often the excuse is given from a misunderstanding of the phrase *joyful noise*. We've all heard it: "It doesn't matter what you sound like, the Bible says to 'make a joyful noise.'" When the Bible uses that phrase, it doesn't mean to make awful music to the Lord. It certainly doesn't mean to give minimal effort to him either.

Psalm 98:4–6 says, "Make a joyful noise to the Lord, all the earth; break forth into joyous song and sing praises! Sing praises to the Lord with the lyre, with the lyre and the sound of melody! With trumpets and the sound of the horn make a joyful noise before the King, the Lord!"

This reference alone describes a joyful noise as a "joyous song," the use of many instruments, and a celebratory song of praise. A joyful noise could also mean a shout of praise, dancing, clapping, etc. Nowhere in Scripture does that term describe a half-hearted attempt at bringing low-quality musical praise to the Lord.

We can, however, find many times when the Bible calls us to pursue excellence in our attempts at anything, especially our worship expressions.

Psalm 33:3 says, "Sing to Him a new song; play skillfully on the strings, with loud shouts." First Chronicles 25:7 notes that the musicians and singers in charge of leading musical worship were "trained in singing to the Lord." Colossians 3:23 charges us to "work heartily, as for the Lord and not for men." First Corinthians 10:31 notes that, "Whether you eat or drink, or whatever you do, do all to the glory of God."

We have sober warnings from Scripture when we don't put forth sufficient effort. Jeremiah 48:10 says, "Cursed is he who does the work of the LORD with slackness." Malachi admonishes the priests of his day for offering subpar sacrifices in worship. He quotes God as saying, "I have no pleasure in you, says the LORD of hosts, and I will not accept an offering from your hand" (Malachi 1:10).

For whatever reason, churches often fall into the same sin pattern of giving half-hearted efforts into their worship ministries.

Excellence: How to Achieve It

Like most good things, excellence doesn't just happen by accident. It's something we achieve by taking several intentional and strategic action-steps.

Planning

There is a school of thought that planning worship and not being free flowing is somehow less spiritual. Many consider that kind of worship to not be "Spirit led." I could argue that the worship leader who spends time throughout the week praying and laboring over their worship planning is spending more time and energy listening to the Spirit's lead than the free-flowing worship leader.

There certainly is a place for spontaneity, and I believe that our churches would benefit from that. But we must not brush off planned worship as unspiritual. After all, God is a God of order (1 Corinthians 14:33), and he brings order out of chaos (Genesis 1).

When planning the elements of worship, think of each of them like a plane that is taking off and landing. Anyone can keep a plane going (at least for a little while) while the plane is in the air. It takes an actual pilot, who is trained and skilled, to successfully maneuver a takeoff and a landing. Many people approach certain spots in our worship gatherings (songs, announcements, prayers, sermons, etc.) like an untrained pilot. They can keep the thing in the air but are clueless as to how to take off or land. We can see this to be true when transitions between spots are sloppy and clearly not thought out or rehearsed. For every element, and every person involved, think through not only what the element is going to be and look like, but think about how to take off and land each segment so that you can smoothly transition into the next. A well-planned worship service will eliminate distractions. Planning has just as much to do with leading worship as standing on stage playing your instrument and singing your song.

Communication

Communication is key. No one is a mind reader. There must be clear communication among staff, worship team members, and the audio/visual team. In our day of digital communication, technology has made it easier to communicate than ever before. So, there really is no excuse for a lack of communication.

There are several tools at our disposal to help us to communicate with our various teams, staff members, and volunteers. Various worship planning software is available and affordable. I also think that it would be helpful for everyone involved in a worship service to have some kind of production meeting beforehand. This is a chance to communicate the plan for the day, coordinate how transitions between segments will be done, ask questions, and iron out any details before the service goes live. Communication will equip the team you lead to show up prepared.

Be Prepared

There are three elements of preparedness necessary for a worship team to achieve excellence. The first element is for the leader to be prepared. They will set the standard for everyone else. When the leader is not prepared, they are not being good stewards of the volunteers' time that they have sacrificed for that ministry. Before the rehearsal and sound checks, the leader must have prepared all chord charts and sheet music, have the stage and instruments set up and in place, and have all dynamics, flow, and transitions prepared and thought through.

The second element of preparedness requires that each instrumentalist and vocalist show up having his or her part learned before the rehearsal. I always know if a new song is going to be rough when I see worship team members listening to them for the first time on their phones as they walk into rehearsal.

The third element of preparedness is being on time. There are some people with no concept of time. And I think the musician/artistic types are more prone to being this way. Being late for rehearsals, sound checks, and even the worship service is damaging to the ministry. First, it's unprofessional. Even if you are a volunteer, you should have a level of professionalism if you are going to commit to anything, especially a ministry. Second, it unintentionally sends a message to the rest of the team that your time is more valuable than theirs. And third, it hinders excellence. We can't give the Lord our best effort if we aren't even going to start out on time.

As a leader, you must set the example for punctuality. I have heard of choir rehearsals starting fifteen–twenty minutes late because the worship leader is still printing off sheet music for everyone. I know of worship teams sitting around on a Sunday morning waiting for the worship leader to finally arrive. I know of a pastor who missed his cue in the worship service because he was in his office on a non-emergency phone call. The team you lead will likely always follow the example of the leader. If they are lax about pursuing excellence and being on time, then the team and the church will as well.

Be Willing to Say "No" to People

Leaders can't be "yes" men/women. We are called and placed in leadership to make difficult decisions, even those that might unintentionally hurt someone's feelings. Just because someone wants to be on stage and showcase what they perceive as musical ability, that doesn't mean we should comply. If we are going to lead worship with excellence, we need to make sure that the right people are in the right place.

As the leader, you may have to refuse a team-member hopeful because of a lack of talent. Every Christian is a worshiper. I would say that God is just as pleased at the heartfelt, tone-deaf praises of the average congregant. But there is a standard of skill that God expects from those who lead musical worship. Those who are lacking the talent may need a period of vocal or instrumental lessons. Maybe you need to give them measurable goals before joining the team, and maybe they simply won't ever have musical talent. The leader must be honest with them.

You may have to say "no" to a potential member not because they lack talent, but because they lack effort. Maybe they aren't committed to rehearsals, punctuality, or preparedness. This level of effort is best suited for a garage band or for being a living room rock star. They shouldn't be given a platform in a worship setting.

You also may have to say "no" to someone because of a lack of humility. This is possibly the most difficult because it has to do with the heart. And because they lack humility, they will likely not see what you see or be willing to follow your leadership. This could also be difficult because they could be incredibly talented. It can be challenging to turn away their valuable talent because they can be a valuable asset to help you achieve excellence. But it's possible that their pride will be the very thing that keeps you from achieving excellence as a team. How does a lack of humility negatively affect excellence? They are likely not willing to learn, because in their minds they've already "arrived." They might have a problem following your leadership. This could cause discord within the team or, at the very least, keep you from moving forward as a unit.

They could also tend not to work well with others. An incredibly talented but prideful person likely won't help you elevate others. They could have the tendency to believe their team members are beneath them. I know of a talented musician who refused to play in the orchestra at their church because it had high school members on the team and her excuse was she didn't like playing with mediocre musicians. Ironically, she claimed to have a passion about discipleship, but, unfortunately, her lack of humility meant she didn't want to lower herself to help elevate others.

Sacrifice

Excellence doesn't happen by accident. It also doesn't come easily. It takes sacrifice; excellence will cost you something.

The project management triangle is a useful visual tool that helps to communicate that we all want projects (or worship services) to be of good quality, and we want to accomplish them quickly and inexpensively.

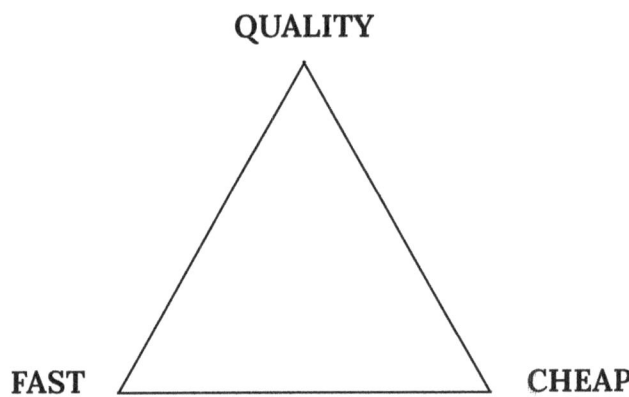

The problem is, we often have to choose only two of these characteristics. In other words, if we value fast and cheap the most, we will sacrifice quality. If we want inexpensive excellence, it will not come quickly. And if we want quality and want it quickly, it won't be cheap.

We have a biblical mandate for excellence. So, you need to figure out what other element you are willing to give up. Many churches will have to reevaluate their annual budget to properly fund the most public ministry in the church. If they simply can't do that, they need to understand the time sacrifices that it will take to achieve excellence on a shoestring budget.

We all have musicians and singers that we look up to. It would be easy to get discouraged about how we can't play guitar, sing, or lead worship like other people. But God hasn't called you to be someone else. He has called you to be the best worship leader, musician, or singer that YOU can be. He has uniquely created and gifted you for a specific purpose to accomplish specific things in specific areas of ministry. For years the United States Army had a great recruitment slogan: "Be all you can be." For us in the Lord's army, our slogan should be: "Be all that God made you to be."

Discussion Questions

1. What has been your understanding of the phrase "joyful noise?"
2. Why do churches often give mediocrity a platform and not demand a level of excellence?
3. Why is excellence important?
4. How would you describe excellence for your local church's worship culture?
5. What are some practical steps that your church must take to achieve the next level of excellence?

Chapter 10
Purposeful Prayer

The worship gatherings of God's people have always been prayerful. The Old Testament saints were faithful to prayer. The Psalter was not only a book of songs but also functioned as a prayer book.

The early church was devoted to prayer (Acts 1:14; 2:42). In most circumstances you could find them praying (Acts 12:12; 14:23). Paul noted his desire for believers "...that in every place the men should pray" (1 Timothy 2:8). Paul encourages the church at Colossae to "Continue steadfastly in prayer" (Colossians 4:2) and the church at Thessolanica to "Pray without ceasing" (1 Thessalonians 5:17).

The worship gatherings of the Old Testament saints and early New Testament saints were filled with intentional, purposeful prayer. Unfortunately, prayer in many worship gatherings today is hurried, unfocused, and often used as a cheap segue, serving as a tool for transitions rather than an element of worship. Hughes Old says, "If public prayer is to be recovered as a meaningful part of the Christian life, considerably more time, thought, and preparation needs to be given to it."[32]

The Model Prayer of Jesus

In just one chapter Jesus provides a wealth of instruction on the act of prayer. Though usually called "The Lord's Prayer" in the Matthew 6 and Luke 11, I prefer the lesser known title of "The Model Prayer." I prefer this wording because Jesus gives us an outline for how we are to pray.

Before he gives the model prayer, he provides preliminary instruction: "And when you pray, do not heap up empty phrases as the Gentiles do, for they think that they will be heard for their many words. Do not be like them, for your Father knows what you need before you ask Him" (Matthew 6:7–8).

"Empty phrases" can also be translated as "meaningless repetition." This also means idle, thoughtless chatter.[33] Can we be guilty of this "meaningless repetition" in our personal and public prayers? Absolutely!

How many of us have heard people mumble, ramble, or speak robotic clichés during prayer? How many times have you seen someone in a worship gathering be called upon to pray for a specific thing and their rambling prayers are so directionless that they end up praying for everything else under the sun? Or have you heard someone who excessively uses God's name in vain: "Dear Father God, we just ask you, Father God, that you bless us, Father God, and that you be our Father, Father God, and our God, Father God."

When our prayers are unfocused and inconcise, we are in danger of heaping up "empty phrases." These thoughtless chatters could reveal that we honor the Lord with our lips, but our hearts are far from him (Matthew 15:8). Our prayers should be intentional and purposeful.

Regardless of your denomination or worship tradition or preferences, I encourage all believers to embrace a more liturgical approach to corporate prayer. This is essentially what the model prayer is. Jesus says: "Our Father in heaven, hallowed be your name. Your kingdom come, your will be done, on earth as it is in heaven. Give us this day our daily bread, and forgive us our debts, as we also have forgiven our debtors. And lead us not into temptation, but deliver us from evil" (Matthew 6:9–13).

So, what does this outline teach us about prayer?

"Our Father . . ."—This speaks of our intimacy with God. We can approach him as his children. God is relational.

". . . in heaven . . ."—Though we are close to God as a Father and child, this phrase still acknowledges his authority as Almighty God of the universe.

". . . hallowed be your name . . ."—In prayer we are to honor the name of God. This is worshipful. We don't go right into our wish list or needs. We pause. We honor our relationship with God, we acknowledge his authority, and declare the greatness of his hallowed name.

". . . Your kingdom come, your will be done, on earth as it is in heaven . . ."—This again acknowledges God's authority. It's also a prayer that is longing to see God's sovereignty fully displayed.

". . . Give us this day our daily bread . . ."—It is good and right to pray to God for him to meet our needs. It acknowledges that all things come from him and that he is our Provider. But this comes after we worship and praise him for who he is.

". . . forgive us our debts . . ."—This is a prayer for forgiveness and reconciliation to God. This is certainly necessary for a thriving worship relationship with God.

". . . as we also have forgiven our debtors . . ."—This is a prayer for forgiveness and reconciliation to others. Also necessary when worshiping our Lord with fellow believers.

". . . And lead us not into temptation, but deliver us from evil."—This is a prayer for holiness and obedience, necessary life characteristics for a worshiper of God.

If we don't actively try to grow and expand our worship and prayer language, our prayers can become stale and routine. We can find ourselves guilty of what Jesus warned against in Matthew 6.

Hughes Old says, "A full diet of Christian prayer naturally includes lamentations, confessions of sin, supplications for forgiveness, and petitions for the gifts of the Holy Spirit."[34] Do we have a "balanced diet" in regards to the different kinds of prayers we pray on Sunday morning or in our personal lives? Do all of our prayers seem to fit one "genre"? Here are some different types of prayers that are often used in worship liturgy.

Prayer of Invocation

Hughes Old best defines this kind of prayer when he says, "This invocation names the God to whom the prayer is addressed. One might therefore define an invocation as a prayer that begins worship by calling on God's name. The Latin word *invocare* means to call upon, to appeal to, or to invoke in prayer."[35]

Many psalms begin with an invocation. Psalm 8:1 says, "O LORD, our LORD, how majestic is your name in all the earth! You have set your glory above the heavens." Psalm 113:1–3 offers a longer invocation: "Praise the LORD! Praise, O servants of the LORD, praise the name of the LORD! Blessed be the name of the LORD from this time forth and forevermore! From the rising of the sun to its setting, the name of the LORD is to be praised!" This is consistent with the model prayer, which begins with an invocation: "Our Father in heaven, hallowed be your name" (Matthew 6:9).

What better way of beginning our worship gatherings than to pray a prayer invoking the name of God?

Prayer of Confession

How many churches neglect clear teachings on sin and repentance? How many churches speak much about sin, but only sins of outsiders and not sins from within? A prayer of confession trains the worshiper to practice a lifestyle of confessing and repenting of sin.

The Book of Common Prayer provides the following prayer of confession:

Almighty and most merciful Father,
we have erred and strayed from thy ways like lost sheep,
we have followed too much the devices and desires of our
own hearts,
we have offended against thy holy laws,
we have left undone those things which we ought to have done,
and we have done those things which we ought not to have done.
But thou, O Lord, have mercy upon us,
spare thou those who confess their faults,
restore thou those who are penitent,
according to thy promises declared unto mankind
in Christ Jesus our Lord;
and grant, O most merciful Father, for his sake,
that we may hereafter live a godly, righteous, and sober life,
to the glory of thy holy Name. Amen.[36]

Prayers of confession give the worshiper a language of confession and a spiritual "muscle memory" to confess and repent of sin. To forsake sin is necessary for churches to worship the way God deserves.

Prayer of Illumination

Gathered worshipers have always prayed some sort of illumination prayer before the reading, teaching, and preaching of the Word. After Nehemiah led the people of Israel to rebuild the city wall, Ezra proclaimed God's Word to the people.

Before he read from the Scripture, he prayed: "And Ezra opened the book in the sight of all the people, for he was above all the people, and as he opened it all the people stood. And Ezra blessed the Lord, the great God, and all the people answered, 'Amen, Amen,' lifting up their hands. And they bowed their heads and worshiped the Lord with their faces to the ground" (Nehemiah 8:5–6).

It makes logical sense that we would pray and ask God to bless his word and to reveal its truth to us since the Holy Spirit inspired Scripture: "no prophecy of Scripture comes from someone's own interpretation. For no prophecy was ever produced by the will of man, but men spoke from God as they were carried along by the Holy Spirit" (2 Peter 1:20–21). It also makes good sense that we pray and ask these things of the Holy Spirit since he also is specifically the one who leads us to understand it. John 16:13 says, "When the Spirit of truth comes, he will guide you into all the truth."

When we pray prayers of illumination over the Word of God, we are acknowledging one of the jobs of the Holy Spirit, and we are trusting in him to do his work.

Note this great Illumination Prayer by Ulrich Zwingli which is based on psalm 119:

Almighty, eternal and merciful God, whos Word is a lampu unot our feet and a light unto our path, open and illuminate our minds that we may purely and perfectly understand Thy Word and that our lives may be conformed according to what we rightly understood, that in nothing we may be displeasing unto Thy Majesty, through Jesus Christ our Lord. Amen.[37]

Many pastors often pray to begin their sermon. Because of habit or tradition, many congregants, or even the pastor himself does not realize that they are praying a prayer of illumination. But when we pray prayers of illumination over God's Word, we are teaching the congregation about this role of the Spirit, and we are communicating that something significant is about to happen when we read, preach, and listen to the Scriptures being taught.

Communion Prayer

Having a communion prayer is as old of a tradition as communion itself, perhaps even older. We are told that after Jesus instituted the Lord's Supper they sung a hymn together (Matthew 26:30 / Mark 14:26). This hymn could have very well been Psalm 113–118, which is known as the *Hallel*, a Jewish prayer that was traditionally prayed together after holidays and celebrations, and especially the Passover. More specifically, during the Supper we are told that he "blessed" the bread and "gave thanks" over the cup (Matthew 26:26–27 / Mark 14:22–23). Luke 22:17–19 records Jesus giving thanks individually over both the bread and the cup.

This tradition has continued on throughout the history of the church. The Book of Common Prayer contains a communion prayer:

> We do not presume to come to this thy Table, O merciful Lord, trusting in our own righteousness, but in thy manifold and great mercies. We are not worthy so much as to gather up the crumbs under thy Table. But thou art the same Lord whose property is always to have mercy. Grant us therefore, gracious Lord, so to eat the flesh of thy dear son Jesus Christ, and to drink his blood, that we may evermore dwell in him and he in us. Amen.[38]

The ancient Didache contains a communion prayer over the cup:

We give thanks to thee, O Holy Father, for thy Holy Name which thou didst make to tabernacle in our hearts, and for the knowledge and faith and immortality which thou didst make known to us through Jesus thy Child. To thee be glory for ever. Thou, Lord Almighty, didst create all things for thy name's sake, and didst give food and drink to men for their enjoyment, that they might give thanks to thee, but us hast thou blest with spiritual food and drink and eternal light throught thy Child. Above all we give thanks to thee for that thou art mighty. To thee be glory forever. Remember, Lord, thy Church to delvier it from all evil and to make it perfect in thy love, and gather it together in its holiness form the four winds to thy kingdom which thou has prepared for it. For thine is the power and glory forever. Let grace come and let this world pass away. Hosanna to the God of David. If any man be holy, let him come! If any man be not, let him repent: Maranatha, Amen.[39]

Having a Communion Prayer as a consistent part of our liturgy is a good practice because we are following biblical example, and keeps the act from being thoughtless and hurried

Prayer of Thanksgiving

A prayer of thanksgiving, or a prayer of gratitude, is often given after the worshipers partake of communion. It is an appropriate response after partaking of the Eucharist in rememberance of the broken body and spilled blood of Christ.

The following prayer of thanksgiving is based on Psalm 116:

Gracious you are, O Lord, righteous and merciful.
Indeed you have dealt with us bountifully.

We walk before you in the land of the living.
Although we have suffered distress and anguish, we have kept our faith.
We are your servants, the children of your handmaiden, the sons and daughters of your Church.

What shall we render unto you, O Lord,for all your bounty to us?
We will take the cup of salvation and call upon your name.
We will pledge to you our lives and all that we are.
We will dedicate ourselves to Christ, our crucified and risen Savior.

For it is in his name that we pray, and in his name that we glory, now and ever more. Amen.

Prayer of Benediction

Closing a worship service with a benediction has been a tradition since the Old Testament. One that was used then, and that many churches still use now, comes from Numbers 6:24–26:

The LORD bless you and keep you;
The LORD make His face shine upon you, and be gracious to you;
The LORD lift up His countenance upon you, and give you peace.

There's something significant about God having the final words of a worship gathering. We don't have to think of something clever or epic to close a service. We could never be so creative that we outshine the Scriptures. Allow your congregation to hear God speak through his Word from the beginning of the service right up until the time that you finish and send them home.

Do written prayers, prayer books, and liturgical scripts seem inauthentic and robotic? They certainly could get that way if we don't gaurd our hearts and actions against it. But our spontaneous, unscripted prayers can certainly become inauthentic and robotic just as easily. Using scripted prayers, even if it's just on occassion, helps us to stretch our prayer launguage. If this is not part of your worship tradition, it would be beneficial to you and to your church to start implementing this practice, even sparingly. This will enhance this element of worship in your congregation, which will further help you develop the overall health of your worship culture.

Discussion Questions

1. How important is prayer in our worship?
2. Does the way you use prayer in your worship gatherings reflect its importance?
3. How have you seen prayer used wrongly in worship gatherings?
4. How can you improve and be more intentional with the element of prayer in your worship gatherings?

Chapter 11
Generous Giving

G iving has always been part of the worship culture of the Christian church. Acts 2:45 notes the early Christians "were selling their possessions and belongings and distributing the proceeds to all, as any had need." Most of them didn't have great wealth. Most didn't have lucrative jobs or prestigious positions. For the most part, Christianity was a blue-collar movement. But even though most weren't wealthy, they were all faithful givers who worshiped the Lord through their generosity.

So, what happened? What is the state of giving in the average professing Christian in America?

American Christians and Their Giving Habits

America is the richest nation in the world. We are extremely blessed by God. But have we (collectively and individually) been good stewards of that blessing?

According to studies, about 19 million Americans are richer than 99 percent of the rest of the world. That's not most of us. But if you have about $4,000 to your name, you are wealthier than half the global population.[40]

The website nonprofitsource.com provides sobering and convicting statistics on the state of giving among American Christians today. Only 5 percent of Christians are tithing (giving 10 percent back to the Lord), and of those, 80 percent only give 2 percent of their income. For families making $75,000 a year, only 1 percent give a tenth to their local church. The average Protestant adult in the United States is only giving about $17 a week. As if that's not sobering enough, non-believers seem to be more generous than Spirit-filled believers. Seventy-five percent of non-Chrsitians donate to nonprofit organizations every year.[41]

Why is this the case? Why are believers today, who are in the wealthiest nation on earth, not as generous as we should be? What is keeping us from being faithful givers? I would argue that we are narcissistic, self-serving, and materialistic.

We can see this to be true because of the amount of debt that we, as a nation and as individuals, are drowning in. At the time of this writing, the national debt is at $26 trillion. The senate is debating right now about adding another $3 trillion to that. As far as personal debt goes, Americans collectively have about $4.1 trillion in consumer debt.[42] One in ten adults carries a credit card balance of $5,000.[43] Student loan debt is plaguing our country, with $1.64 trillion of collectie debt and the average American having $35,000.[544]

Unfortunately, debt is a way of life in America. This greatly affects our ability to give. But I don't think the debt is necessarily the problem as much as it is the symptom. We are in crippling debt because we are selfish and greedy. We want to have nice things, and we live beyond our means. So giving is not something that many *can* do, and we are not generous.

Much repentance needs to be made as a nation, as a church, and you and I as followers of Christ if we are to be faithful to worship God through giving. The truth is, money is either an object *for* worship or it will be an object *of* worship.

The Bible sternly warns against the failure to give. In Malichi 3:8–18 the people of Isreal were rebuked for not giving the full tithe. They were accused of "robbing God." That's a pretty serious accusation. Likewise, Acts 5 tells the story of a man named Ananias who sold some property, only gave a portion of what he should have, and was dishonest about it. Because of this, the man died.

God takes giving seriously. Unfortunately, most believers in the United States do not. Many are guilty of robbing God of what is rightfully his. And they are robbing themselves of the joy of worshiping him through their generosity.

The Bible on Giving

The Bible has much to say on the subject of financial stewardship, generosity, and giving. It is a subject that is covered extensively in both Testaments. Over two thousand verses in Scripture address money and giving.

Giving in the Old Testament

The tithe, as far as we see in Scripture, originated with Abraham in Genesis 14:8–20. The tithe was clearly commanded several times throughout the Old Testament law. Leviticus 27:30 notes that this is a holy commandment: "Every tithe of the land, whether of the seed of the land or of the fruit of the trees, is the Lord's; it is holy to the Lord."

Deuteronomy describes this command in detail as a holy act of worship: "When you come into the land that the Lord your God is giving you for an inheritance and have taken possession of it and live in it, you shall take some of the first of all the fruit of the ground, which you harvest from your land that the Lord your God is giving you, and you shall put it in a basket, and you shall go to the place the that the Lord your God will choose, *to make His name dwell there*...And you shall set it down before the Lord your God. And you shall rejoice in all the good that the Lord your God has given you and to your house...This day the Lord your God commands you to do these statutes and rules. *You shall therefore be careful to do them with all your heart and with all your soul*" (Deuteronomy 26:1–2, 10–11, 16, emphasis added)

Proverbs 3:9 states: "Honor the Lord with your wealth and with the firstfruits of all your produce." By properly stewarding our wealth and giving generously, we are honoring the Lord; we are using it to worship Him.

Jesus on Giving

Jesus spoke more about money than any other topic. More than sin, heaven, or any moral issue, Jesus spent a great amount of time addressing the topic that consumes most of our mental, emotional, and even physical energy.

I was once on staff at a church that decided to do something out of the ordinary for us: a four-week sermon series on money, stewardship, and giving. After two or three weeks, there were talks and accusations that all we, as pastors, wanted to talk about was money. This was ludicrus because none of the three of us preaching during that series had ever preached a sermon specifically on giving before. And to be honest, if we were to follow Jesus's example of preaching, we should have been doing more of that all along. Most pastors aren't greedy charlatans like the crooked televangelists or prosperity preachers. Most of them are underpaid and underappreciated, trying to do the best job they can to serve the Lord and his church. If you accuse your faithful pastor of only wanting to talk about money, that probably says more about the idolatry in your heart than it does about the sermons in the pastor's pulpit.

Here are some of the principles that Christ taught us about worshipful giving.

Give Sacrificially

Mark 12:41-44 records the story of Jesus observing the giving of a poor widow: "And he sat down opposite the treasury and watched the people putting money into the offering box. Many rich people put in large sums. And a poor widow came and put in two small copper coins, which make a penny. And He called His disciples to Him and said to them, 'Truly, I say to you, this poor widow has put in more than all those who are contributing to the offering box. For they all contributed out of their abundance, but she out of her poverty has put in everything she had, all she had to live on.'"

Did this woman give 10 percent of what she had? No. She gave it all. She gave sacrificially. All of the excuses that professing Christians make for not faithfully giving seem like rubbish compared to the faithfulness of this woman. She was a widow, so she had no husband to provide financially for her. Back then they didn't have life-insurance policies or 401ks. It's likely that she was elderly, so on top of being a female, tshe was further limited in her ability to earn a living. Yet still she gave. She gave all she had because she worshiped the Lord, not her money. She worshiped the Provider and not the provision.

Give in Secret
In Matthew 6:1–4 Jesus notes: "Beware of practicing your righteousness before other people in order to be seen by them, for then you will have no reward from your Father who is in heaven. Thus, when you give to the needy, sound no trumpet before you, as the hypocrites do in the synagogues and in the streets, that they may be praised by others. Truly, I say to you, they have received their reward. But when you give to the needy, do not let your left hand know what your right hand is doing, so that your giving may be in secret. And your Father who sees in secret will reward you."

When we give, we are not to make a show out of it. We aren't to post it onto social media. If we make significant contributions to the church's building fund, we aren't to have the building named after us. We are to give in secret. Only God, and maybe the recipient, should know about it. We are to give without expectations of favors, status, or power.

Don't Be a Slave to Money

In the story of the Rich Young Ruler, Jesus converses with a young man who had great wealth. He approached Jesus wanting to know how to inherit eternal life. Jesus conftonts him over his possessions, calling on the man to forsake them and follow him. The man refused. Jesus comments to his disciples: "It is easier for a camel to go through the eye of a needle than for a rich person to enter the kingdom of God" (Mark 10:25).

Jesus wasn't saying that if you have wealth you are going to hell. In this context, Jesus was pointing out the fact that this young man thought he owned great wealth, but the reality was, the wealth owned him.

In Luke 16:13 Jesus states: "No servant can serve two masters, for either he will hate the one and love the other, or he will be devoted to the one and despise the other. You cannot serve God and money."

Do we own money, or does it own us? We are to rule over our money and not allow it to rule over us. It is to be stewarded, not served. We can't be generous people and worship God with our money if it is our money we are really worshiping.

Giving in the New Testament

When we, as New Testament believers, worship through giving, where is that money supposed to go? Doesn't this make church too much like a business? The truth is, God has mandated that the Christian give in order to financially support certain things for his kingdom.

There are a few things that Scripture commands believers to financially support through their giving. The first is pastors and ministry leaders. First Timothy 5:17–18 says, "Let the elders who rule well be considered worthy of double honor, especially those who labor in preaching and teaching. For the Scripture says, 'You shall not muzzle an ox when it treads out the grain,' and 'The laborer deserves his wages.'" Like the Philippian church supporting Paul's missionary efforts (Philippians 4:16–20), we too are to financially support mission efforts. We are to feed the hungry and provide for the needy (Acts 4:23–35), especially widows and orphans (James 1:27).

In 2 Corinthians 9 the apostle Paul provides incredible instruction for worshipful giving in the life of a New Testament follower of Christ. His doctrine of giving goes beyond a 10 percent tithe. He admonishes the saint to give out of abundance: "Whoever sows sparingly will also reap sparingly, and whoever sows bountifully will also reap bountifully. Each one must give as he has decided in his heart, not reluctantly or under compulsion, for God loves a cheerful giver" (verses 6–7).

There are several things to unpack in these two verses. First, Paul notes that each person must give "as he has decided in his heart." This seems to imply that giving is not bound by the tithe. This is consistent with the rest of the New Testament, such as the previously mentioned widow and her two coins (Mark 12:41–44), or what Paul said in the previous chapter about how the Corinthians, though they were in poverty, still gave generously. So, unlike the average professing Christian in America, this giving "as he has decided in his heart" is not a free pass to give little but is rather a charge to give abundantly.

Paul also notes that we are not to give "reluctantly or under compulsion." Not reluctantly, out of guilt. The ministry leader is not to shame his people into giving, for that does not produce true, joyful generosity. God is not glorified as much as he deserves from that kind of giving. And there is no real reward for the giver who only does so out of guilt or obligation.

The believer is also not to give under compulsion. Though there is a time for spontaneous giving, that shouldn't be what the majority of our giving looks like. Our giving should be budgeted, planned, and strategized. It should be calculated, scheduled, and consistent. Does that seem unspiritual to you? Does it take away the fuzzy feelings when we get calculators and calendars involved in giving? I would argue that a strategic, budgeted, and planned giving strategy is far more spiritual than giving on a whim. Think about it. When we strategize our giving, we spend a lot of time planning on how we are to give. We make adjustments to our weekly, monthly, and annual lifestyles. This is truly dying to yourself in order to glorify God, bless others, and be filled with joy.

When we give freely, not reluctantly, and when we give strategically, not under compulsion, we can become what Paul calls a "cheerful giver." This term "cheerful" literally means that we are "hilarious givers." It communicates that we are in abundance of joy as we are able to give. Each month when we sit down with our budget and figure out how we can make our money stretch in order to give, we can be that "cheerful giver" because we know that we are giving abundantly but also are still able to pay the light bill.

Many believers may be fearful of growing in this area of their worship life. Maybe you have never been taught to be a faithful giver. Perhaps you had no one to show you how to make a budget and stick to it. So, maybe you know that you need to begin to give more than you do, but you are fearful of how you can make your dollars stretch enough to pay your bills.

Paul offers some encouragement: "And God is able to make all grace about to you, so that having all sufficiency in all things at all times, you may abound in every good work. As it is written, 'He has distributed freely, he has given to the poor; his righteousness endures forever. He who supplies seed to the sower and bread for food will supply and multiply your seed for sowing and increase the harvest of your righteousness. You will be enriched in every way to be generous in every way, which through us will produce thanksgiving to God" (2 Corinthians 9:8–11).

We must remember that God will provide the means of generosity. We just have to be faithful. If we seek to live a generous life, be good stewards of what he has given us, and commit to a life of worshipful giving, God will provide all of our financial needs. You may have to give up some of your "wants" or luxuries. I've found that when I'm more focused on the Lord and being a good steward of *his* money, I'm not as concerned about all of the extra luxuries that I don't really need.

I love how Paul closes his admonishment on giving: "Thanks be to God for His inexpressible gift" (verse 15). We are able to give because God is the ultimate giver. He gave us life. He gave us good gifts. He gave us his Son. We can't become generous people by our own strength because we are selfish creatures by nature. But when we fix our hearts on the fact that God gave us his inexpressible gift of Christ, we are empowered to become generous, cheerful, *hilarious* givers.

Discussion Questions

1. What are some of the reasons for a lack of giving among believers?
2. Does God still expect a 10 percent tithe, or should we give beyond that?
3. How does your debt affect your ability to worship through your generosity?

Chapter 12
Singing

When most of us think of worship, we usually think about singing. In fact, many people define worship by using some kind of musical term or reference. Though worship isn't exlusively musical or the act of singing, it is a significant element of worship and a necessary element for a healthy worship culture.

Mike Cosper said, "Our faith is a sung faith. The people of God sing in war and peace, victory and defeat, celebration and lament. On the one hand, our singing is otherworldly. We sing an ancient song that climaxes in the hazy but hope-filled future. We sing as living people among the walking *dead*."[45]

Worship through singing is a big deal. It is important and should be treated as a priority in the life of every church.

Why Do We Sing?

Christians sing becasue our theology mandates that we do. All throughout Scripture we see examples of worshipers singing. After crossing the Red Sea, Moses writes and teaches a song for the Israelites to participate in (Exodus 15). Jesus sang with his disciples (Matthew 26:30). The apostle Paul sang (Acts 16). The largest book in the Bible (Psalms) is a collection of songs.

We have glimpses of heaven that describe angels surrounding the throne of God saying in unison, "Holy, holy, holy" (Isaiah 6:3; Revelation 4:8). It is easy to believe that these words are being sung. Eternity will be filled with singing saints (Revelation 7:9-11).

We sing because God said so. Over one hundred times in the Psalms alone, and more times throughout the rest of Scripture, God commands his people to sing. Like a great leader, God not only gives us a command, but he leads by example. Zephaniah 3:17 notes God singing: "The LORD your God is in your midst, a mighty one who will save; he will rejoice over you with gladness; he will quiet you by his love; he will exult over you with loud singing." Hebrews 2:12 notes Jesus continuing to sing praises to the Father: "I will tell of your name to my brothers; in the midst of the congregation I will sing your praise."

What Does Singing Accomplish?

It's clear in Scripture that Christians are supposed to sing. We know this because of clear instruction and many examples provided for us. Knowing that we should sing is easy. But why? *Why* do we sing? What does it accomplish? There are many things throughout Scripture that show us what congregational singing accomplishes.

Singing God's Word Helps Us to Remember God's Word

Colossians 3:16 notes: "Let the word of Christ dwell in you richly... singing psalms and hymns and spiritual songs, with thankfulness in your hearts to God." Singing has a significant impact on our memory. That's why when you sing God's Word, the word will "dwell in you richly." Churches would do well to sing portions of God's Word. Not only is it a beautiful thing to sing God's Words back to Him, but you will remember those words all of your life.

Singing Teaches and Admonishes

Colossians 3:16 also notes another purpose of congregational singing: "*teaching* and *admonishing* one another in all wisdom, singing psalms and hymns and spiritual songs, with thankfulness in your hearts to God" (emphasis added). Teaching God's truth and stirring the worshiper to obey it are central to the Christian faith (James 1:22). Singing about such things cements them into our hearts and minds.

Singing Evangelizes

In Acts 16 Paul and Silas were imprisoned for preaching the gospel. Verse 25 notes that they spent the evening singing: "About midnight Paul and Silas were praying and singing hymns to God, and the prisoners were listening to them." I find it interesting that Luke added the little detail that "the prisoners were listening to them." This would be significant because of how the story pans out. God sent an earthquake that freed all of the prisoners (verse 26). Because this would certainly be a death penalty for the guard, he was about to take his own life. Paul stopped him from doing so and shared the gospel with him. That man and his entire household came to faith in Christ (verses 30–34). Singing is an incredibly effective tool for evangelism. Though I believe that the worship service is for the saints to participate in, we would be foolish not to try to be good stewards of those in our services who do not know Christ yet. Our singing needs to be clear about the sinfulness of man, the death and resurrection of Christ, and God's call for the sinner to repent and place faith in Christ.

Singing Stirs Our Emotions

Music taps into a person in a way that nothing else can. God has created us with emotions and feelings. Unfortunaly, some churches actively try to supress emotions. I don't find that to be biblical, logical, or healthy. God intends for us to use our emotions and feelings in a healthy way that glorifies him. That's why Jesus told the woman at the well that true worshipers will worship in spirit and truth (John 4:24).

Singing Is Prayer

Worship theologian Constance Cherry notes singing as a "sung prayer" when she says, "Corporate worship services, in their entirety, are in themselves one large prayer that worshipers offer to God. The whole liturgy *is* prayer in the sense that it consists of God and people in conversational relationship."[46]

We certainly are to sing songs *about* the person and work of the Triune God, but we must not forget to sing songs *to* him as well. Our worship must be relational. We must think about it as a dialogue between us and God. God speaks to us through his Word and we speak to him by singing songs of praise to him.

Singing Unifies

Singing is one of the few things that we can do collectively. There are even fewer things that we can do collectively and in unison. But singing is one of those things. Singing is meant to unify the Body of Christ as we collectively sing truths to and about God that we agree with and have united around.

It's unfortunate that this thing that God meant to unify his people has been used to cause division. Fight against that. Surrender your preferences to one another. Stand together as a unified people and sing with confidence about the Risen Savior that unites and binds all believers!

How Do We Foster a Culture of Singing?

How does a pastor, a worship leader, or a church leader help foster a culture of singing at their church? Here are some qualities that our songs must have to accomplish this.

Diversity Your Songs

Both Colossians 3:16 and Ephesians 5:19 instruct us to sing "psalms and hymns and spiritual songs." There is debate over the nuanced differences between the three, but the point is to diversify. Different genres of songs accomplish different things. An exclusively psalm-singing church is commendable, as they are singing God's Word, but they are failing to embrace other kinds of worship songs that the Bible not only gives us liberty to participate in but also instructs us to do. Likewise, churches that only sing hymns are missing out on testimonial songs or newly written songs. These churches that are exclusively hymn-singing churches are wrong in believing that one specific song genre from one general time period is acceptable in worship. And churches that are exclusively contemporary that never sing hymns or participate in psalm singing are missing out on some incredibly enriching songs of praise. Bottom line, if it is doctrinally sound, sing it. God will be pleased and the church will be enriched.

Sing Singable Songs

Is there a memorable melody to the song? That's one of the qualities of a great song. It can have incredible lyrics, but if it's unsingable because the melody is too complicated or too bland, then it will be nearly impossible for the congregation to learn it, own it, and participate in it.

Likewise, is the song in a singable key? Most of our congregants are not going to be trained or experienced singers.

Make sure that the songs aren't in a key that's too high or too low for the average person to sing.

Now, what determines whether or not a song is too high or too low will differ among cultures, age demographics, and styles of music. For example, in the days of Johnny Cash, singing in a lower key was far more common in popular music. In the 1980s, rock singers were singing such high notes; most of us can't follow along with them.

Worship leaders often sing in keys too high for the congregation to follow. However, this is not exclusively a modern worhsip issue. There are many hymns in the hymnal that are in an uncomfortable key for me. The modern worship era often gets blamed for this issue because we are just more aware of this today than during the era of only hymns.

It's a difficult balance for the worship leader to find the right key for a song to be able to sing comfortably and confidently and be able to be heard while also choosing a key that will be comfortable for the average congregant. Try to have a pastoral approach to this. Your selection of keys is a shepherding opportunity. You can set your congregation up to follow you if you have theire abilities and/or limitations in mind.

Sing at a Reasonable Volume

Yes, we can make a biblical case for loud worship. Psalm 33:3 references new songs, skillful strings, and loud shouts. But we would be foolish to think that volume can't become a distraction for worship.

It's important to keep in mind that, like many things, what determines whether or not something is too loud or not loud enough varies between different age demographics, churches, cultures, and people groups. Becuase of my demographic and temperment, I like loud music. But I'll never forget going on a mission trip to the Dominican Republic. The main thing I observed from that culture is that they tolerate a louder volume than we do. As the mission team arrived at the airport, the church had chartered a bus for us. We had to drive for a couple of hours to reach our destination. The bus had a TV on which they played a movie, but the volume was blaring and piercing. As we arrived at our destination, I noticed that car stereos weren't regulated by any volume laws. And when we had worship services in the local pastor's living room, the house and congregation were small enough that there was no reason for a sound system, but they used one anyway. The pastor cranked up his microphone and preached his heart out. All of that was totally acceptable in that particular culture but would be considered unpleasant for most people in America.

There is no perfect volume level. You have to find out what works best for your local body. Make sure your music and sound system are not the ultimate things. They are just tools to achieve a higher goal. They are a means to help congregations worship through participatory singing.

A church should be a singing people. A worshiping church will be a singing church. Make this a priority if you want to foster a healthy worshp culture.

Discussion Questions

1. What has been your most significant experience of singing in worship?
2. Why do you think God has commanded us to sing?
3. What does congregational singing accomplish?
4. What can you do to foster a culture of singing in your church?

Chapter 13
Inclusion of People

G od loves when his people gather for worship. There are good reasons for the Bible to be so explicit about the expectation for Christians to worship Christ in a group. Christian worship gatherings always work best when believers gather not to spectate but to actively participate and to lead.

Inclusion of Participants

Corporate worship gatherings were always meant to be participatory. From the sixth century to the Reformation, Christian worship gatherings were largely a spectator's event. For most worship gatherings, only clergy or singers approved by the clergy sang. Every element of worship was done by the clergy, and often in Latin, and the congregants passively observed.

The Reformers made intentional efforts to lead the worship of the church back to a particapatory act. Much work, sacrifice, opposition, and persecution was endured to bring congregational worship back to the people.

There is, and always will be, a "togetherness" in Christian worship practices. Note the wording in the following verses:

addressing **one another** in psalms and hymns and spiritual songs . . . submitting to one another out of reverence for Christ. (Ephesians 5:19, 21, emphasis added)

Let the word of Christ dwell in you richly, teaching and admonishing **one another** in all wisdom, singing psalms and hymns and spiritual songs. (Colossians 3:16, emphasis added)

Let us consider how to stir up *one another* to love and good works, *not neglecting to meet together*, as is the habit of some, but encouraging *one another*, and all the more as you see the Day drawing near. (Hebrews 10:24–25, emphasis added)

And they devoted themselves to the apostles' teaching and *the fellowship*, to the breaking of bread and the prayers. . . . And all who believed *were together* and had all things in common. . . . And day by day, attending the temple *together* and breaking bread in their homes, they received their food with glad and generous hearts. (Acts 2:42, 44, 46, emphasis added)

Corporate worship was never supposed to be about an "audience of one." While we are only worshiping God, we are mindful of God's people. Pastors and worship leaders would do well to include as many participatory elements of worship in their gatherings as they can. These can include partaking of communion often, corporate prayers, congregational Scripture readings, and songs that are in a style, tempo, and key that encourages participation.

Inclusion of Servant Leaders

Throughout Scripture, particularly in the Old Testament, we find the model for worship leading to be a group effort. King David recruited 288 skillful musicians and singers to be used in leading musical worship (1 Chronicles 25:7). Nehemiah recruited 245 singers (Nehemiah 7:67), and likewise Ezra recruited 139 Levites and singers (Ezra 2:40–41) to lead worship.

Worship leading is not like preaching a sermon. We who lead in musical worship depend on a team, an army of people to achieve our ministry goal. Ecclesiastes 4:12 says, "Though a man might prevail against one who is alone, two will withstand him—a threefold cord is not quickly broken." Bottom line: when we work for God's kingdom, we accomplish more when we work with God's people.

If we are going to be faithful leaders in the church, we can't hoard all of the leadership tasks and opportunities to ourselves. Ephesians 4:11–12 says, "And he gave the apostles, the prophets, the evangelists, the shepherds, and teachers, to equip the saints for the work of the ministry." Our role as pastors and worship leaders is not to do all of the work of the ministry but to train up faithful believers to help us lead. This is an essential part of discipleship. If you are the worship pastor or musical director, your job is not only teach to your people how to be participants of worship, but you are also to teach your people how to be leaders of worship.

How can you properly utilize willing participants and give them opportunities to lead and to serve? I would make a case that worship teams shouldn't be an exclusive club. I don't believe it should be all-inclusive, but I also don't believe it should only be for a select few. You may consider having worship-leading events, venues, and opportunities for all age groups, such as children's worship choirs and worship bands and choirs for teenagers. I would even invite those young leaders to help lead in the main service(s) on Sunday. I believe all-age worship bands and choirs are a beautiful thing to see on a Sunday morning. Some of my most blessed experiences as a worship leader are having singers and musicians who are pre-teenagers sharing the platform with singers and musicians who are senior adults. It communicates that every age group is valued and capable of leading the body of Christ in worship. There could be worship-leading opportunities for the Christian who isn't necessarily musically gifted. I would encourage pastors to allow their congregants to lead in times of congregational prayer, publicly read Scripture, give words of testimony, baptize new believers, and administer the Lord's Supper. There's nothing in the Bible that forbids a layman from doing so.

The more people you include and develop as servant-leaders, the healthier your church's worship culture will become. The reality is, this doesn't come without challenges. The more people you include, the more opportunities for conflict, sin, and difficult personalities you will have to navigate.

When dealing with difficult people and the conflicts that will arise, it's important to always be reminded of the leadership example that Christ set for us. Philippians 2:1–8 outlines his perfect example of humble, servant leadership:

> So if there is any encouragement in Christ, any comfort from love, any participation in the Spirit, any affection and sympathy, complete my joy by being of the same mind, having the

same love, being in full accord and of one mind. Do nothing from selfish ambition or conceit, but in humility count others more significant than yourselves. Let each of you look not only to his own interests, but also to the interest of others. Have this mind among yourselves, which is yours in Christ Jesus, who, though He was in the form of God, did not count equality with God a thing to be grasped, but emptied Himself, by taking on the form of a servant, being born in the likeness of men. And being found in human form, He humbled Himself by becoming obedient to the point of death, even death on a cross.

Likewise, Peter exhorts church leaders to "Shepherd the flock of God that is among you, exercising oversight, not under compulsion, but willingly, as God would have you; not for shameful gain, but eagerly; not domineering over those in your charge, but being examples to the flock" (1 Peter 5:2–3).

The worship leader's team will make them or break them. If a church is going to have a healthy worship culture, you will need a unified army of God's saints to help you carry that burden. So, treat them well.

God's vision for your church's worship culture is for everyone to participate together in passionate expressions of praise, fixated on his Person and his work. It's up to you to unite the body of Christ around this vision. It's up to you to lead them to participate and to train others to lead with you.

Discussion Questions

1. How can you foster a worship culture that includes participation rather than observation?
2. What are some practical ways that your church can raise up servant leaders in your worship culture?

Chapter 14
Worship as a Lifestyle

In the previous chapter I discussed how a church with a healthy and vibrant worship culture functions with the inclusion of people, both in participation and in those that lead and serve. Another element of a healthy worship culture is not what takes place when the church is gathered but when they are scattered, as the congregants practice a lifestyle of worship. Christian worship is not only public, but most of it is (or should be) private. Rory Noland says, "The first step to becoming a better worshiper is to become a vibrant worshiper Monday through Saturday. As believers, we can worship God on our own, one-on-one, and experience the power and privilege of worship every day."[47]

The apostle Paul instructed New Testament believers in a lifestyle of worship when he said, "I appeal to you therefore, brothers, by the mercies of God, to present your bodies as a living sacrifice, holy and acceptable to God, which is your spiritual worship" (Romans 12:1). He uses imagery of a sacrifice, which his readers would have been familiar with. He notes that we don't present out bodies as an act of worship by offering ourselves as a slain offering, but we are a sacrifice of worship that is *living*.

He further elaborates on how we function as a living sacrifice of worship: "Do not be conformed to this world, but be transformed by the renewal of your mind, that by testing you may discern what is the will of God, what is good and acceptable and perfect" (Romans 12:2). We live a lifestyle of worship when we walk in obedience and holiness, seeking to bring honor to God in everything that we think, do, and say. When we choose to abstain from sin, he is glorified. When we repent of sin in the ways that we fall short, the Lord is honored.

Worship is not bound by a location or a church building. It is not bound by a specific day or time, such as Sunday mornings. It is not bound by a certain expression, like music. Worship is a lifestyle because, by nature, we are worshipers.

King David is one of many who set a great example of what it means to be a lifestyle worshiper. In Psalm 34 he wrote: "I will bless the LORD at all times; His praise shall continually be in my mouth" (verse 1). He goes on: "Oh, taste and see that the LORD is good! Blessed is the man who takes refuge in him!" (verse 8). He recognizes that God is worthy of continual praise. Be it with his fellow worshipers, or all alone, David worshiped.

Jesus, as he does with all good things, showed us what it meant to practice a lifestyle of worship. As a boy, he loved worshiping at the temple (Luke 2:41–52). As a faithful Jewish man, he consistently attended services at the temple (Luke 21:37). He observed the Passover with the disciples (Luke 22:7–13). Often, he would go off alone to pray (Matthew 4:1–2; 14:1–13; Mark 6:30-32Luke 5:16).

So, how do we do this? Practically speaking, what are some ways that the believer in Christ can grow as a private worshiper? How can a pastor and worship leader foster a healthy worship culture by training their members to be faithful worshipers seven days a week? Here are some important principles to develop a worship lifestyle.

Lifestyle Worship Must Be Made a Priority

Growth as worshipers won't happen by accident. It will take intentionality. It will take sacrifice. It must be important enough to arrange our priorities and our schedules to make it an active and consistent part of our personal lives. Most people claim that they simply don't have time for prayer, Bible study, and other forms of private worship.

The truth is, we make plenty of time, even an excessive amount of time for things that aren't really all that important. How much time do you spend on your phone? Most people spend an average of three to four hours per day on it.[48] One study shows that the average adult in America spends about thirty-eight minutes per day scrolling through social media, while sixteen–twenty-four-year-olds spend a staggering three hours per day.[49] John Piper once said, "One of the great uses of Twitter and Facebook will be to prove at the Last Day that prayerlessness was not from a lack of time."[50] What's even more convicting about this is that while we spend so much time on our phones to the neglect of spiritual disciplines, many of us believers have some kind of Bible app right next to our social media apps.

What about television and Netflix? About 140 million hours of content per day is consumed on Netflix, and the average American consumes about 19.6 hours per week and 2.8 hours per day watching television or other streaming platforms.[51] The CEO of Netflix, Reed Hastings, said that their biggest competition isn't Amazon, YouTube, or even traditional cable, but it was sleep.[52] That's why the platform is formatted for binge watching.

It's not that we lack time for private worship, it's just that we don't make time for it. It's not a priority for many Christians. This was not the case with David. In Psalm 27:4 he said, "One thing have I asked of the LORD, that will I seek after: that I may dwell in the house of the LORD all the days of my life, to gaze upon the beauty of the LORD and to inquire in His temple." The "one thing" that David wanted in life was to be a worshiper of God.

I encourage all believers, as we make a worship lifestyle a priority in our lives, to have a standing appointment with the Lord. We all have standing appointments in our lives, be it something that happens every day, every week, or every month. These are important things that we know will consistently happen. They are so important that they take priority in our schedules. Every other activity, goal, or project is scheduled around these most important appointments. We need to do the same with our appointment with God. If we make our meeting with him a top priority, we will schedule it and work everything else around it.

When making these standing appointments, it is important that they are scheduled in a time of day when you are most functional. If you, like me, are not a morning person, don't feel guilty because legalism tells you that our meeting with God has to be early in the morning. I'm definitely more of a night owl. I love the quiet stillness of night. All the hurry of life has settled down and I can really focus my heart. Some may prefer the morning, some may prefer the evening, some may prefer their lunch hour. It doesn't matter when you meet with God. Just be consistent and choose a time when you can give him your full attention.

The most fruitful time for you may change depending on your season of life. For example, I used to always have my main worship times and Bible studies in the evenings. Then, my wife and I started having kids. I would then find myself, as all parents to little ones do, exhausted by the time the sun went down. During that time, I would prepare to read Scripture, and I could barely keep my eyes open, much less give my full attention. I floundered like that for months before I realized that was no longer a fruitful time for me. Early in the morning was still no good, but I found that about 7:30am was a perfect time for me for a while. Now that my kids aren't babies anymore, but they are still young enough for an 8:30 bedtime, evenings are once again my sweet spot. Figure out when your standing appointment works best for you, when you are able to give God your full attention, free from distractions.

Lifestyle Worship Is a Spiritual Discipline

Words such as "habit" or "routine" as they relate to worship usually describe worship that is stale, empty, or heartless. While that can certainly be true, these aren't necessarily bad words to use to describe the lifestyle worshiper. In fact, they are necessary. Having a consistent habit and routine means you are disciplined, and worship is a spiritual discipline. David was a disciplined worshiper. In Psalm 145:2 he notes his daily practice of worship: "Every day I will bless you and praise your name forever and ever."

To grow in this spiritual discipline and for our worship to become habit forming, I've found two specific things to be very helpful on top of having a standing appointment with God. The first thing is to have a plan. Zig Ziglar famously said, "If you aim at nothing, you will hit it every time." While he wasn't talking about spiritual disciplines, the principle can still be applied here. For your worship plan, you may aim to read through specific parts of Scripture. You may work through memorizing a book of the Bible. Maybe you want to sing through an entire hymnal in a year. Or you may have a prayer list that guides your worship time. These are only a few suggestions. Find out what your soul needs the most in any given day or season. Form a plan. This plan will help you grow in consistency.

Second, I advocate that we make technology work *for* us, not *against* us. Entire books can be written about how technology is a massive distraction in our lives. We all know that we can be, and to some extent are, slaves to our technologies. I encourage you to not be ruled by it but to rule over it. There are apps that have every version of the Bible ever made. You can have entire commentary sets at your fingertips. Perhaps you commute to work. Use this technology to redeem your drive time by listening to an audio Bible app. One way that I love to make my smartphone work for me is by using it to set reminders. You can set it to remind you of your standing worship appointment. There may be a specific prayer need that you would like to be praying about at a certain time of day. Set your phone to alert you to pause, reflect, and pray. We don't have to let our technology create undisciplined Christians. Rule over it. Be its master so that your heart can focus on *the* Master.

Lifestyle Worship Happens in All of Life's Moments

If I were to ask you to describe your most significant worship experience, what would it be? For most of us, we would probably describe a public gathering of some sort. For me, I think of my first time at a Passion conference in Atlanta, Georgia. It was 2006, and I was in my second year of college. It was the first time that I had ever witnessed that many people gather together in one place to praise the name of Christ. It was nothing short of phenomenal.

There's nothing wrong with thinking about large events as being among the most impactful times of worship that we've ever had. We crave big experiences. We want to experience the *Shekinah* glory. We love conferences, camps, and retreats. Sound systems, bands, and lights can be used to lead us well. These are all great times, places, and tools for worship, but they aren't the only times and places that we can experience significant worship moments.

Part of practicing a lifestyle of worship means that we learn to worship in the ordinary moments. The day-to-day, seemingly mundane things that we experience can and should be moments that tune our hearts to God. Paul says in 1 Corinthians 10:31, "So, whether you eat or drink, or whatever you do, do all to the glory of God." Even our most mundane tasks, such as eating or drinking, should be acts of worship. Everything that we do, every day, every moment of our lives, we should be seeking to glorify and worship the Lord. The key is to notice these seemingly mundane things and see the common-grace gift from God that they are.

One thing that I've done with my children is to take little things that they love and teach them to be in awe of the God who gave them. For example, my kids love candy. I mean, they *really* love candy. This is fresh on my mind because all three of them had dentist appointments today, and, miraculously, none of them had cavities. But on occasion as I saw them eating sweets and living in absolute bliss, I would ask them: "Do you like that candy you're eating." Emphatically, they would shake their heads and scream: "YES!!!" Then I would respond with, "How awesome is God, that he would give us candy? How great is he that he would give us a tongue to be able to taste it? That's pretty great for God to do that, right?" Then we would say a little prayer of thanksgiving over God's good and perfect gift of . . . candy. My goal with that little exchange is to teach them to savor the little moments of life and for them to practice worshiping in the ordinary, everyday moments of life.

When Christians are vibrant worshipers Monday through Saturday, churches will experience white-hot worship on Sunday mornings. Church leaders must commit to fostering and training their congregants to not only worship when they are gathered but also when they are scattered. Then we will see revival. Then we will see transformation. And God will be worshiped as he deserves.

Discussion Questions

1. What does a worship lifestyle look like for you?
2. What would Sunday morning worship look like if everyone practiced a lifestyle of worship?
3. How can church leadership help believers grow in the spiritual discipline of practicing a worship lifestyle?

Endnotes

1. Harold Best, *Unceasing Worship: Biblical Perspectives on Worship and the Arts*, (Downers Grove, IL: InterVarsity Press, 2003), 18.

2. Wayne Grudem, *Systematic Theology: An Introduction to Biblical Doctrine*, (Grand Rapids, MI: Zondervan, 1994), 1003.

3. Evelyn Underhill, *Worship*, (London: Nisbet, 1936), 61.

4. Mike Harland, *Seven Words of Worship: The Key to a Lifetime of Experiencing God*, (Nashville, TN: B&H, 2008).

5. Vernon M. Whaley, *Called to Worship: From the Dawn of Creation to the Final Amen*, Nashville, TN: Thomas Nelson, 2009), xviii-xix.

6. Ibid. xviii-xix.

7. Ibid. xviii-xix.

8. Ibid. xviii-xix.

9. Franklin M. Segler and Randall Bradley, *Christian Worship: Its Theology and Practice*, (Nashville, TN: B&H, 2006), 3.

10. Bes, *Unceasing Worship*, 21.

11. John Piper, *Let the Nations Be Glad: The Supremacy of God in Missions*, (Grand Rapids, MI: Baker Academic, 2003), 17.

12. "If Only Oprah Knew God's Jealousy Was Anthropomorphic," YouTube Video, :59, August 9, 2011, https://www.youtube.com/watch?v=n2SrZJlPnjk

13. J.I. Packer, *Knowing God*, (Downers Grove, IL: InterVarsity Press, 1973), 170.

14. Bob Kauflin, *Worship Matters: Leading Others to Encounter the Greatness of God*, (Wheaton, IL: Crossway, 2008), 155.

15. John MacArthur, *The MacArthur New Testament Commentary: Matthew 8-15*, (Chicago, IL: Moody, 1987), 283.

16. Lisa Green, "Why 734 Pastors Quit (and How Their Churches Could Have Kept Them)," *Christianity Today*, January 12, 2016, https://www.christianitytoday.com/news/2016/january/why-734-pastors-quit-how-churches-could-have-kept-them.html.

17. Gary Harbaugh, *Pastor as Person: Maintaining Personal Integrity in the Choices and Challenges of Ministry*, (Minneapolis, MN: Augsburg Fortress, 1984), 47.

18. David Murray, *Reset: Living a Grace-Paced Life in a Burnout Culture* (Wheaton, IL: Crossway, 2017), 39.

19. Murray, *Reset*, 39.

20. John MacArthur, *Worship: The Ultimate Priority*, (Chicago, IL: Moody, 2012), 153.

21. Rory Noland, *Worship on Earth as It Is in Heaven: Exploring Worship as a Spiritual Discipline*, (Grand Rapids, MI: Zondervan, 2011), 147.

22. Bryan Chapell, *Christ-Centered Worship: Letting the Gospel Shape Our Practice*, (Grand Rapids, MI: Baker Academic, 2009), 116.

23. Walter A. Elwell, *Evangelical Dictionary of Theology*, (Grand Rapids, MI: Baker Academic, 2001), 705.

24. Justin Martyr, *The First Apology of Justin*, (Chapter 68).

25. Segler and Bradley, *Christian Worship*, 25-26.

26. Lester Ruth, Carrie Steenwyk, and John D. Witvliet, *Walking Where Jesus Walked: Worship in the Fourth-Century Jerusalem* (Grand Rapids, MI: Eerdmans Publishing, 2011), 24.

27. James F. White, *A Brief History of Christian Worship*, (Nashville, TN: Abingdon Press, 1993), 85.

28. White, *A Brief History of Christian Worship*, 88.

29. White, A *Brief History of Christian Worship*, 90.

30. White, A *Brief History of Christian Worship*, 90.

31. Robert E. Webber, *Worship Old and New*, (Grand Rapids, MI: Zondervan, 1994), 111.

32. Hughes Oliphant Old, *Leading in Prayer: A Workbook for Worship*, (Grand Rapids, MI: Eerdmans, 1995), 361.

33. John MacArthur, *The MacArthur New Testament Commentary: Matthew 1-7* (Chicago, IL: Moody, 1985), 368.

34. Old, *Leading in Prayer*, 77.

35. Old, *Leading in Prayer*, 11.

36. Episcopal Church. *The Book of Common Prayer and Administration of the Sacraments and Other Rites and Ceremonies of the Church : Together with the Psalter of Psalms of David According to the Use of the Episcopal Church.* (New York, NY: Seabury Press, 1979).

37. Gottfried W. Locher, *Zwingli's Thought: New Perspectives*, (Leiden: Brill, 1997), 28.

38. Episcopal Church, *The Book of Common Prayer*.

39. George Cantrell Allen, *The Didache: Or, the Teaching of the Twelve Apostles*, (London: Astolat Press, 1903).

40. Kathleen Elkins, "How Much Money You Need to be Part of the 1 Percent Worldwide," CNBC, 1 November 2018, https://www.cnbc.com/2018/11/01/how-much-money-you-need-to-be-part-of-the-1-percent-worldwide.html.

41. "Church and Religious Charitable Giving Statistics," *Non-Profit Source*, https://nonprofitssource.com/online-giving-statistics/church-giving/#:~:text=The%20average%20giving%20by%20adults,giving%20by%2020%25%20or%20more.

42. John C. Heath, "2020 Consumer Debt Statistics," *Lexington Law*, 19 February 2020, https://www.lexingtonlaw.com/

blog/loans/consumer-debt-statistics-2019.html#:~:text=Average%20revolving%20debt%20per%20capita,%243.089%20trillion%20in%20November%202019.

43. Megan Leonhardt, "55% of Americans with Credit Cards Have Debt—Here's How Much it Will Cost You," CNBC, 17 May 2019. https://www.cnbc.com/2019/05/17/55-percent-of-americans-have-credit-card-debt.html.

44. Travis Hornsby, "Student Loan Debt Statistics in 2020: A Look at the Numbers," *Student Loan Planner*, 14 November 2020, https://www.studentloanplanner.com/student-loan-debt-statistics-average-student-loan-debt/#:~:text=Student%20Loan%20Debt%20Statistics%20in%202020%3A%20A%20Look%20at%20The%20Numbers&text=Borrowers%20in%20the%20U.S%20owe,to%20the%20Department%20of%20Education.

45. Mike Cosper, *Rhythms of Grace: How the Church's Worship Tells the Story of the Gospel*, (Wheaton, IL: Crossway, 2013), 152.

46. Constance M. Cherry, *The Music Architect: Blueprints for Engaging Worship in Song*, (Grand Rapids, MI: Baker Academic, 2016), 45.

47. Rory Noland, *Worship on Earth as it is in Heaven: Exploring Worship as a Spiritual Discipline*, (Grand Rapids, MI: Zondervan, 2011), 14.

48. Adrienne Matei, "Shock! Horror! Do You Know How Much Time You Spend on Your Phone?," *The Guardian*, 21 August, 2019, https://www.theguardian.com/lifeandstyle/2019/aug/21/cellphone-screen-time-average-habits#:~:text=According%20to%20research%20from%20RescueTime,four%20and%20a%20half%20hours.

49. Denis Metey, How Much Time Do People Spend on Social Media?," *Review* 42, 21 November 2020, https://review42.com/

how-much-time-do-people-spend-on-social-media/#:~:-text=The%20average%20US%20adult%20spends,was%20 142%20minutes%20a%20day.

50. John Piper (@JohnPiper), "One of the greatest uses of Twitter and Facebook will be to prove at the Last Day that prayer-lessness was not from a lack of time," *Twitter*, 20 October 2009, https://twitter.com/johnpiper/status/5027319857?lang=en.

51. Michelle Castillo, "Netflix Only Takes Up 8 Percent of the Time You Spend Watching Video, But the Company Wants to Change That," CNBC, 17 July 2018, https://www. cnbc.com/2018/07/17/netflix-small-portion-of-overall-watch-time-and-competition-is-stiff.html#:~:text=GBH%20 Insights'%20internal%20research%20found,hours%20a%20 day)%20for%20comparison.

52. Aatif Sulleyman, "Netflix's Biggest Competition is Sleep, Says CEO Reed Hastings," *Independent*, 19 April 2017, https:// www.independent.co.uk/life-style/gadgets-and-tech/ news/netflix-downloads-sleep-biggest-competition-video-streaming-ceo-reed-hastings-amazon-prime-sky-go-now-tv-a7690561.html

Made in the USA
Las Vegas, NV
27 April 2022

48092031R00111